HAIRPINS & HAPPINESS

A Hairstylist's Guide to Building a
Successful Bridal Business

Carleana DeLaCruz

CONTENTS

PRELUDE:

My Story

I am a product of the late 1990's, a time of chunky highlights and tiny, glittery butterfly clips. Those aren't the only things that have since gone in and out of style. Back then, there was an ideal timeline for growing up and being successful - go to college, get a degree, get a 'good' job with a briefcase, blah, blah, blah.

So, I enrolled at our local community college to go out and make something of myself.
I hated it.

I did, however, learn two things:

1. I thrive in a creative environment.
2. I did NOT want to be stuck behind a desk day in and day out.

Every time I left a class I thought, "Oh, my gawd. I have to come back on Wednesday?"

I hated the commute. The parking. The homework. Everything. I pulled decent grades and liked the one interior design class I was taking, but aside from that? Meh.

College clearly wasn't for me, but I felt stuck with no direction.

I worked a few part time jobs while continuing the mundane community college life, but nothing worth mentioning. Then, I got a call to be a model for a major hair care line at a hair show in Detroit, Michigan. Before you roll your eyes at my humblebrag, please note that being a hair model just means I happen to have the right hair texture and length for what they're planning on teaching.

I jumped at the opportunity!

The gig was going to pay $200 whole dollars *and* I got my haircut and colored for free?! Plus, it was the day of my 19th birthday?! My teenage heart fluttered with excitement! Best job evvveerrrr!!

Backstage was a chaotic circus of costume fittings, hair coloring, clouds of aerosol hairspray, model walk practicing, avant-garde wigs, and all the trappings! The static noise was heavy with female voices, water splashing at shampoo bowls, the whirrrr of multiple blow dryers, and the clicking of high heels on the ceramic tile floor.

All the models had to sign a contract specifically stating what the different hair care companies were allowed to do with their hair. Some models' contracts were cut and/or color only, and others were to demonstrate braiding techniques. I wanted to keep my nearly waist length hair "ponytail-able' but they could color it any way they saw fit.

The way they colored my hair backstage was very subtle and enhanced my natural dirty blonde tones. I had a special scenario where my haircut was to be done live on stage in front of nearly 1000 hair stylists. We were told before going on stage, "No matter what happens, hold your head high and just smile."

The stage lights were blinding and had the heat of an oven. If you've ever been on a stage before, you understand the oddity of knowing everyone is fixated on you, despite you not really being able to make out any faces. The audience was entranced by the techno beat blaring while making the occasional 'oohh's' and 'aahh's' in echoed unison. My haircut was rocked out center stage by a hairstylist that was self-admittedly "heavy handed."

The stylist was razor cutting my wet hair to the beat of the music. She thrusted my head left, then right and pushed my hair forward in my face. I kept a slight smile plastered and my eyes closed as she continued thrashing through my hair with her comb and blade. With each beat hair flew every which way. She forced my head down where I opened my eyes slightly to discover about two feet of my hair length in my lap.

Just smile.

After the whirlwind cut she removed the styling cape with a single whoosh and, much like a magician, presented her masterpiece to the audience. Just as quickly as we had begun, we were done.

My heart was pounding with both fear and excitement. I sat on a stool to the side, no longer the center of attention but still smearing the same forced smile across my teeth, wondering what was left of my hair. (Remember, the audience was my mirror. I could not see myself anywhere from the stage.)

Roughly an hour later, AKA the longest hour of my life, I left the stage to see the result. I went into a dimly lit broom closet they called a bathroom to catch a glimpse of my reflection. I barely recognized myself.

I had a mullet. I had full, thick bangs. I had a soccer mom fringe that started behind my ears and reached the high point of my head shape then came forward straight across my brows. None of my friends or peers had bangs in 2002. The severe side bang of the early 2000's was about to become all the rage, but hadn't quite busted out yet in the Midwest.

Here's the thing - the contract I had signed was not broken. I could indeed put the back of my hair in a ponytail. A very shorn, heavily textured, spindly, ponytail.

I never cried. I'm not a crier. Many of the other models sobbed uncontrollably, realizing they should have thought twice about ticking the "do anything to my hair" box in their respective contracts. One doe-eyed fourteen year old's head had been mostly shaved in front of a live audience and what was left was magenta in color. Needless to say, she was so distraught, she didn't go back on stage for the finale. I had learned the power of the "consultation" on that day. Those of us that had asked questions and gave parameters weren't nearly as shocked as those naive, starry-eyed models that gave none.

Despite the carnage, I was hooked. I was dazzled by the energy and passion all the hairstylists had for their craft. I craved more of it.

By the end of the month, I was a proud college dropout, and enrolled in a local Cosmetology school. I was elated, practically foaming at the mouth, to start my new career and passion as a professional cosmetologist!

*Please Note: If while reading anything within the pages of this book something sounds a bit fishy, ignorant or out of place you should probably pause, go back to the beginning of the paragraph and reread it. Please assume it was meant to be read with heavy sarcasm.
You may now proceed.

THE BEGINNING:

But, where do we start??

Firstly, congratulations! If you're reading this book, you have made the first step toward developing your own successful bridal beauty business!

Secondly, you may already be confident that you have what it takes to succeed as a bridal stylist, or you may be hesitant to get into the industry. Either way, if you picked up this book, you are among the few of us stylists that *truly* love bridal work. Many working stylists are intimidated by finishing and formal work. The fact that you are interested in that niche says that you are already on your way to success in the bridal industry.

> ## "Learn the rules like a pro, so you can break them like an artist."
> ## -Pablo Picasso

I'm not going to teach you *how* to do hair and makeup. The purpose of this book is to guide your future success as an artist and a business owner. I *am* going to share how I successfully built my own bridal beauty business.

There are an average of **2 Million** weddings per year in the United States alone. I'm ambitious, but I could never take them all on as clients. There are plenty of weddings to go around and the key is to do our best to streamline and attract the most ideal brides for our own brand.

I want you to be able to learn from my experiences. There are so many questions surrounding the beauty industry. What licenses do you need for which services? Do you need insurance, and if so, what kind? How do you get a foothold on the whole social media thing? Is it possible to seem confident, not cocky? How do you build relationships? What needs to be included in a contract - if you even need one? The list goes on and on. We're going to answer these questions by taking a deep dive into creating bridal contracts, branding, professionalism, marketing funnels, and more fun stuff along the way!

All of this may seem daunting to you. It certainly did to me when I got started in this business. Start by taking one chapter at a time, and then doing one task at a time. Putting the hard work in now sets you up for the rest of your career to become seemingly effortless.

I learned a phrase when I was traveling in Florence, Italy. While I was there, I took a cooking class. Between rolling out the pasta and stirring the sauce, our teacher said, "piano, piano." It roughly translates to, 'take it slowly' or 'step by step' in Italian. Whenever I'm tackling something that seems difficult or tedious, I can hear the sweet, confidence of her Italian accent in my ear, "pee-ahh-noh, pee-ahh-noh." It's like my own little 'whistle while you work' mantra. It's my process, and soon you'll find one, too.

Let's start with a few basic questions...

1. Are you feeling overwhelmed by the thought of starting your own business?
2. Have you recently started your own bridal business, only to feel hopelessly stuck or frustrated?
3. Do you know how to book a bridal party?
4. Who is your ideal bride? Is she a traditional bride with a large bridal party? A BoHo bride who intends to elope?
5. Do you plan to perform bridal services on location or in

a salon setting? Or both?

6. How is your ideal bride going to find you?

Once you've determined some of the specifics of what you're wanting out of your beauty business, you can start moving forward toward the fun stuff!!

"Fun stuff," you ask? Yes, the *fun* stuff!! The things about this industry that get your blood pumping and your adrenaline racing! The projects that you can't wait to sink your teeth into and set your creative soul on fire! Once we have your marketing funnel in place and the above questions answered, we can make room for more of the fun stuff.

Depending on where you are in your career currently, you may not be entirely sure of what sets your soul on fire. That's okay too. I went on quite a journey getting to where I am today. Every deliciously tedious task has major pay off, both creatively and financially. And believe me when I tell you, it feels SO good to get there. To know that you're in the right profession for you and your lifestyle. A sense of peace that only those of us that truly love our careers can really understand. Achieving happiness and success is no small task. It takes a lot of hard work to get there. It takes so many humans a lifetime to get even a glimpse of it.

As professional hair stylists we make our clients feel beautiful. We ensure that our clients love their reflections. Our career is beyond rewarding when you think about the impact that we have on their self-esteem and self worth. The happiness that washes over us when we witness them seeing their own reflection and smiling from ear to ear is unparalleled. We crave more of that feeling and that's what keeps us motivated to do more of what we love!

Get ready, because the entrepreneurial life is a wild ride of ups, downs, challenges, and triumphs. But if you love this industry and the work that you do, it's all worth it in the end!

I'm here to tell you that there is a whole wide world of

possibilities out there just waiting for those of us with enough ambition and guts to take them!

* * *

I didn't always know I wanted to be a *bridal* stylist. I started out knowing I wanted to "do hair," whatever that means. In cosmetology school I quickly worked out that I was not interested in doing facials or mani's and pedi's. I liked the creativity of styling, haircutting, and color. Nails and skin care just didn't give me the same creative charge.

It wasn't until I was nearly done with Cos school that I attended a hair show as a stylist, errrr…. student, for the first time. It was held by one of the Midwest beauty suppliers at the Amway Grand Hotel in Grand Rapids, MI.

All the headliners were, and still are, like rock stars in my eyes. They are the celebrities of our profession.

It was there, in that arena, that I saw Martin Parsons for the first time. He was the Updo Guru in the late 90's and early 2000's. Martin had a ton of VHS tapes (ask your parents what those are) showcasing his elaborate upstyling work and how to achieve it for yourself.

"1,2,3,4,5,6,7,8,9,10,11,12!" If you know, you know!

I was in a trance while watching this hair wizard strategically place his model's hair into elaborate formal styles that, at the time, seemed like only *he* could accomplish.

Leaving that show I knew I wanted to master his techniques. As luck would have it, my cosmetology school had quite a collection of his videos, and I studied them over and over with my mannequin head in front of me. I was forever addicted.

Luckily, my passion introduced me to a lucrative market. Did you know that out of the roughly 500,000 licensed cosmetologists in the United States, less than 20% accept updos and finishing work? Of that 20%, even less of us accept brides and wedding parties, and even fewer **thrive** in the bridal beauty industry due to lack of organization, marketing, and business acumen.

If you're amongst the elite 20%, you are part of a beauty niche that has a ton of potential! We are the coveted few! The wedding industry needs us!

According to The New York Times, over a quarter million weddings took place in 2022. Of those quarter of a million weddings, the average total cost was approximately $29,000. IBIS World Statistics claims that over $60 billion was spent on the wedding industry in 2022, and budgets are expected to grow by an additional 2% annually for the next couple of years.

According to WeddingWire.com the average cost for a bride's hair alone on her wedding day is $300. Some brides pay as little as $100 or as much as $1000+ for their wedding hair and makeup!

That doesn't include the rest of the bridal party, or a bridal preview, which is generally $135-$250 per person. If you own your own company, you have the freedom to charge for your talent and time, and decide how you want to structure bridal hair packages and pricing.

❊ ❊ ❊

Warning: This book is not for you if you're not in an open mindset. Do yourself a favor and close the book now if you are lazy, think you already know everything, or are looking for a fantastical magic wand to remove all the hard work in a single wave.

This book is specifically intended to help guide beauty professionals and help them grow successful beauty businesses, and that requires hard work, positivity, and an open mind. Please close this book now and walk away if you are lazy or a negative Nelly. This book is to be used as a compass not a magic wand. You have been warned.

✲ ✲ ✲

Now that they're gone, let's continue -

I'm sure there are people still here reading this thinking, "I've seen her work, I can do that," or "She isn't doing anything that I can't do," or "anyone can do hair, why do I need this book?" I picture these naysayers thinking these things with the enthusiasm of my twelve year old daughter, accompanied by her trademark over-exaggerated eye roll.

"Either be judged or be ignored."
-Seth Godin

I see you, and here's the thing. You're not wrong. You *can* do what I do. There are plenty of talented stylists out there in the world doing amazing things. I am simply taking the time to sit down and write about them.

I'm fully aware that there are many talented people in the world of hairstyling. Some, I'm sure, are far more talented than I. The difference between all of us doesn't come down to skill level. It comes down to something far more basic. Personal connections and work ethic.

My hope is that some of you reading this are inspired to go out there and make it on your own. Start with the basics of marketing. Start designing the website. Get the professional photos. Do the thing. You are getting ready for your own journey into the world of entrepreneurship and that's really exciting!!

Although this book is not going to teach you *how* to do hair, it will give you an easy to follow road map to help you build a successful bridal hair business. Answer the questions throughout the book and you'll see your very own bridal beauty business start to take shape!

This book and my voice are here for you. Lean into the idea that you can stand on your own and make big things happen for yourself and your business! Just know that it's going to be hard work and it's all worth it!

I am proud of you and you should be too.

Let's get started...

> **Please Note:** While reading this book you may or may not come across some verbiage that you're unfamiliar with. Please take the time to flip to the back of this book's Lingo section to clear up any confusion!*

Homework:

Fill in the blanks-

- What is your current income?
  -weekly average/ monthly average/ year end salary?

- What are your monetary goals for next month/quarter/ year?

- What is your why?
  -Travel? Family? Free time? Money isn't specific enough, we all have jobs.

- What's your personal mantra?

- Research your possible social media handles - search the hashtags, what do you find?

- What does your personal branding look like? -The answers to the following may help you identify your unique branding...
  - Favorite client/service type?
  - Favorite quote?
  - 5 possible professional social media handles for your business?
  - Favorite color?
  - Favorite makeup?
  - Favorite smell?
  - Favorite song?
  - What are your hobbies?
  - What fills your free time?
  - What was the last book you read and enjoyed?
  - Best local restaurant?
  - Last person you hugged?

I know some of these seem silly but they will help you visualize your ideal business imagery. Trust the process.

Goals:
today-
this week-
this month-
this quarter-
by the end of the year I will...

Extra Credit Questions:

- Do you have a marketing funnel in place?

- How is it working?

- Do you see a steady flow of inquiries coming from your marketing funnel?

- When was it last updated?

- What can we do to improve your funnel?
- What products and tools can you not live without?

PROFESSIONAL RELATIONSHIPS:

How to Build them & How to Nurture Them

When figuring out where we should begin this journey into building your bridal beauty business, this in my mind, was the most obvious starting point. I will refer to both professionalism and building professional and client relationships throughout this entire book.

No matter where you are in your career, this is of the utmost importance. If you can't exude confidence and professionalism, you will have trouble in this industry. They may seem harsh but it rings with truth.

It's a personal industry. We are welcomed into the inner sanctum of people's lives when they hire us to take care of their beauty needs on their wedding days. That isn't something to take lightly. We as beauty professionals need to wear many hats.

The owner and CEO hat. The friendly and confident hat. The marketing guru hat. The social media wizard's hat. The clever entrepreneurial hat. The witty, jokester that can bring down the anxiety level in the room by a few decibels, with bells on it, hat. Oh, and remember we should be simultaneously taking care of the beauty needs of the bridal party while wearing all of these many hats!

Gofer is yet another hat we sometimes sport. We are often asked to help out with tasks outside our wheelhouse on the day of an event. I have no problem with this and do not see it as an unprofessional ask. It's often part of the chaos, and I embrace it.

Jump in and help out if a vendor is carrying things in and you're just standing around waiting for the bride to change into her dress. Hold the door, help find the groom's brother for the photographer. So long as it doesn't impede your ability to do your job, step up. It will be noticed and appreciated!

On the other hand, if you decide to be rigid about this topic and not help tie bows on the favors when asked, it will be noticed in a negative light. It's hard to look someone in the eye and say "Nah, not feelin' it" when asked to carry something or hold a door. It's a small gesture, don't get bent out of shape about the silly stuff.

"Go the extra mile. It's never crowded."
-unknown

Because brides don't come into the salon every 4 to 8 weeks for trims and touch ups, it takes a bit longer to build a base clientele for your bridal business.

Although I truly love doing bridal work, I've always kept my cut and color business as well. I have long standing relationships with my clients and they would be impossible for me to send off to other stylists and salons. They are the reason I love my job. They trust me

I know some bridal stylists that do just that. End their long term client/stylist relationships in order to pursue a full-time gig as an exclusive bridal stylist. There is nothing wrong with that. It's, actually, very impressive. It just never felt right for me and my business.

* * *

According to society, on paper at least, hair stylists are paupers.

Hear me out...

Remember earlier when I shared the average wedding cost of 2023 and how less than 20% of stylists accept finishing work and weddings?

As reported by salary.com, the average hair stylist in the United States of America makes an annual income of $28,320 or roughly $15 an hour. That's if you were to work a 40 hour work week and take 2 weeks of vacation (unpaid) per year. That is literally barely above the poverty threshold and *less* than what the average wedding costs. I find this completely unacceptable.

I refuse to be mediocre. You should refuse to be mediocre. That my friends is mediocre pay.

We can all do better and being the professional that I know you are is the first step toward premium pay, for a premium skill set and a premium lifestyle.

We, as professional hairstylists, do not commit our lives to a substandard craft. We are ever evolving, changing and learning. We strive to be the best at what we do because we are not the conventional, struggling stylist. We are the elite. We are the exception to the rule. We are the beauty professionals all others strive to be. We hustle and work for what we have. This is another lesson in the journey toward the career of your dreams....

A major key to building a professional relationship with other wedding vendors is confidence.

There is a difference between cocky and confident.

The cocky stylists are conceited, egotistical and have an arrogant nature that repels instead of attracts. Think of them as the Shooter McGavins of the beauty world. They seem insincere and phony. (and probably have too many teeth and a fake Rolex)

The confident stylists are aware of their successes but don't feel the need to brag or boast. They are forever optimistic and assured of their own capabilities. Think of them as the Mary

Poppins of the beauty world. Devilishly confident and well put together.

Both confidence and cockiness can help you gain great success because at the core they're both assertive. Just promise me that you'll follow through on your commitments and air on the side of Mary Poppins!

There's nothing worse than a cocky stylist that has a false sense of self and can't deliver on their obligations.

"Sure thing! I can run circles around anyone! I'll do the entire bridal party of 12 with one hand tied behind my back, while juggling flaming torches, in less than 4 hours and everyone's hair will be perfect and stay all night long and they'll all love me! Did I mention I'll do all of that barefoot while hula-hooping and walking up hill in the snow?" >insert finger guns and an exaggerated wink here<

Cringe.

As with all things in this life, it's far more impressive to under promise and over deliver.

Zazzle had great success early on in their business because they promised your shoe order in 5 days and you always had them in your hot lil hand by day 3. Brilliant business strategy. They knew darn well that they'd be able to deliver before day 5. They promised a 5 day delivery, knowing they would be able to blow that expectation out of the water. Getting your order to you well before promised was no mistake.

Lesson learned.

Long before an event date I do a little homework. I get on social media and follow all the vendors listed in the wedding agreement. I reach out especially to the wedding planners and photographers. They seem to be the most active on social platforms and photographers have the goods that you need to showcase your work after the event on your own socials.

Zap them a private message. Something short and sweet like,

'Hello Blank! I look forward to working with you on 2/3/24 for the Smith wedding! Let me know if you have any questions about my timeline for the day!'

This achieves three things:

1- You have introduced yourself and exchanged business contacts; which stylists rarely do.
2- You have followed them; which all vendors appreciate.
3- You are proving your professionalism; before you ever meet face to face.

All of these things help you stand out as a leading professional in your area.

On the day of the wedding or event make sure to take flattering behind the scenes photos of other vendors working to post to your stories on social media. Many vendors aren't in front of the camera lens often and appreciate the effort to showcase themselves hard at work for a change.

I'm able to snag the BTS shots by lingering for a bit after my work is complete, but prior to starting clean up. I rarely have time to get my phone out for pictures before all my ladies are taken care of. Doing so could jeopardize the timeline we have in place. Lingering for a few BTS snaps inconveniences no-one and maintains my professionalism.

After you have done all the touch ups, cleaned up and say one more congratulations to the bride, go post to your stories on socials. More often than not I'm doing this step in the venue's parking lot before I even leave the premises!

Note:
When posting your behind the scenes snaps, tag everyone involved, including the bride! (Do not post any behind the scenes shots of the bride *or* her dress until an hour after the ceremony time- nothing makes a bride more cranky than an early reveal!!)

The vendors will see that you've extended this olive branch and will do the same for you. Promise.

Usually, the BTS posting phase lasts a day or two and typically turns into a love fest! All the vendors and bridesmaids will be sharing, liking and following each other and showering each other with compliments and praise.

The photographers typically post a sneak peek on their socials within a day or two of the event. Share them. Always. I don't care whether you post them in stories, reels or to your grids, just make sure to share and tag all vendors and the couple to make sure they receive credit for their beautiful work..

A few days or a week after the wedding date reach back out to the before mentioned wedding vendors via private message. 'Hello again! It was great working with you on the Blank wedding! The sneak peeks are gorgeous! I'd love to see more images of the wedding so I can share your beautiful work on my feed!'

Very seldom has a photographer or videographer not shared images with me as a professional courtesy.

We are all in this together. You scratch their back by tagging them and making their work more visible on social media and they're going to scratch yours right back!

This is how you build a beautiful portfolio of images to then add to your website and marketing. (with the bride and photographer's blessings of course)

Word of mouth and referrals are the backbone of how I've built my business. Unlike building a cut and color clientele, you don't tend to get a lot of repeat business. (notice, I didn't say zero!) However, every bride has a sister, cousin, friend or coworker that's getting married soon. If a bride of yours sings your praises their tribe will hear it. That is the absolute best business builder you can ask for!

Referrals don't just come from happy brides. They often come from wedding vendors that admire your work and work ethic. Make nice with the wedding vendors and you'll start seeing a steady flow of referrals from them as well.

Ask wedding vendors that you enjoy working with if you can add them to your 'Preferred Vendors List' on your website. They are usually flattered and extend the gesture back to you as well. Think about it: If a couple comes to them asking for referrals they must trust that vendor's opinion. You are automatically in a trusted inner circle, just because you're on that list.

Small acts of kindness within the wedding vendor community will help give you traction in your quest to build the bridal business of your dreams. Exchanging business cards, following and staying active on other vendor's social media, adding vendors to your Preferred Vendors List; all these little things add up big time. They give you a strong foothold amongst your local wedding vendors. Eventually, this can spread regionally and so on.

The potential is truly limitless. My hope is that you will take this knowledge that I'm currently sharing and one day surpass my successes. When that happens I can start learning from you!

Approximately a week or two after the event date, send a follow up to your bride. Just a sweet and simple 'Congratulations, you made a beautiful bride' email, text or private message is perfect.

Again, this helps you stand out in the crowd. This is a final step that most hair stylists and makeup artists do not take. This is one of those small, seemingly inconsequential, details that take a hair stylist to the top tier, elite. I know it sounds silly. It's not.

As I mentioned before, brides don't come into the salon every 4 to 8 weeks for trims and touch ups, so it takes a bit longer to build a base clientele for your bridal business than it will to book regular cut and color clientele.

Be patient but persistent. My first year behind the chair I booked 2 weddings total. Now, at the time of publication in 2023, I have to put a cap on how many I'll accept, which is between 15 to 20 annually.

If you grind and work hard, it will pay off. Look for open doors and walk through them.

> "If you don't go after what you want, you'll never have it. If you don't ask, the answer is always no."
> - Nora Roberts

I learned this concept from my entrepreneurial husband very early in our relationship. He is in sales and obviously applies this theory to his business daily. He has proven this theory time and time again.

His mantra is the abbreviated version: "If you don't ask, the answer is always no." but just as effective as Ms. Roberts'.

If you don't ask for the referral, you won't get the referral.

If you don't ask if a photographer wants to collaborate, they'll never know you're interested.

See my point?

Early on in my husband and I's courtship we took a long weekend trip to Chicago. (a very MidWest thing to do) When we pulled up to our hotel's valet, the stoic attendant informed us that there was zero parking available for valet and that we would need to take our sorry keisters six blocks away to self park.

My then 21 year old boyfriend stepped out of our vehicle with authority, looked over his shoulder at me and said with a wink, "I'll be right back."

He walked over to speak to the valet attendant one on one with the stride and confidence of a career politician. They spoke for a few minutes like old friends. Laughing and gesturing toward the cars and building with an occasional nonchalant wave.

To be 100% honest, I have no idea exactly what was said between the two of them as I watched from the passenger's seat. What I do know is that when he strolled back and climbed into the truck he had a proud grin on his face.

I watched in confusion as the attendant got into another car parked in front of the valet stand and pulled it out into the street, straddling the curb. I was even more tongue tied when my boyfriend then pulled our truck into that exact spot once filled by the attendant's vehicle.

Both men hopped back out of their respective vehicles and gave a firm hand shake. My future husband attempted to hand him cash for a tip. The valet attendant put his hand up and shook his head no as a denial of the monetary exchange.

The next thing I heard was "Thanks, man." as my boyfriend returned to our vehicle. He then opened the driver's side door once more and said with a huge, toothy smile spreading from ear to ear, "We're all set. Let's go check in."

I was dumbfounded.

"What did you say to him?" I stammered.

"The answer is always no, if you don't ask." was all he would tell me.

I later found out that the valet attendant had actually moved his own vehicle for us to take his personal parking spot *and* that we didn't end up paying for the valet service at all. We literally went from walking 6 blocks in the dark and paying city parking prices, to sauntering in from the front curb for zero payment.

Now, I hope that you're not thinking that EVERY ask will end up in a positive outcome with rose petals thrown at your feet. Sometimes the answer is 'not right now'. Let it sit and come back to the question at a later time. Questions often turn into opportunities when they're revisited.

If the answer is a firm no, learn from it. Was it a no from that dream photographer that you're dying to work with because your business esthetics didn't align with theirs? Did you not sound confident when you approached them? Did you not have enough experience?

Move forward. Assess the situation and ask another photographer to collaborate. Or another client for a referral.

Eventually, you will get a yes. Build from there.

* * *

Get published, featured, and advocate for yourself...

Now that we know about building professional relationships and nurturing those connections let's dive into publication.

It is a huge professional triumph to have your work featured and published in magazines, print advertisements and on social media, blogs and podcasts. Potential brides and other professional wedding vendors often find you this way. It also immediately gives you authority and credit in your professional niche, putting you on a higher tier than your competitors and peers.

More often than not when I have had my work published and featured it was spearheaded by the project's photographer or event planner.

The before mentioned vendor submitted a press kit or other submission to the magazine that sometimes includes but is not limited to a collection of photos, the full list of professionals that helped bring the shoot or event to life, and the backstory and inspirations behind the overall theme.

On the rare occasion I have asked for permission from the main vendors of an event to submit for publication. Some magazines and wedding sites have a 'submit for publication' link. There is typically a form of basic questions to fill out and then a space to download the appropriate files and photos. (make sure to pay attention to what format and sizing is required for submission or you will be automatically denied. PDF and JPEG are most common.)

As in all things in this life we have to make sure to advocate for ourselves, our work and what we believe in. Sometimes things all fall into place and other times we need to do a little leg work to make sure there is follow through on other professional's part.

I previously mentioned reaching out to other vendors and industry professionals. ..

I'll never forget the day I opened up the email from a nationally published bridal magazine.

It was a normal day off. I had a load of laundry started, I had just dropped off my daughter at preschool and was settling in on the sofa at home to check work emails and do any billing that needed tending to. Nothing extraordinary, but all necessary.

While scrolling through my emails I came across it. It was a congratulations letter from a nationally published bridal magazine that shall remain nameless. (Let's reference it as NPBM for the purpose of this story and anonymity.)

I held my breath with excitement while combing through the lengthy email. My mouth was gaping open and my fingers and toes were tapping with anxious enthusiasm! My work was to appear in the 'Real Brides' section of their spring publication!! This was the first time I had ever had a publication reach out to me instead of the other way around. They found me to clarify how I wanted to be credited in the print and online versions of the magazine. They reached out to me!? Whhhaaat!!?? This only happens in hairstylist's dreams, right?? This is a feeling reserved for the rock stars. For the Hollywood, uber famous. Not little ol' me.

But it was, it was meant for me and my work and I was elated!!

I responded promptly with my salon contact information and address as well as my personal Instagram and Facebook (This was circa 2012 - I didn't have a website or any professional social media handles and still worked for a commission based salon back then) They sent a very formal confirmation of the details and included the projected publishing dates.

And now we wait…

It was agonizing to know I was about to have my work in print. In a real magazine that is nationally recognized. Every week seemed to crawl at a tortoise's pace. Each month was a countdown, bringing me closer and closer to the big finally!!

When the long awaited day came, I went as quickly as I could to the local Super Mart's magazine rack, and scoured the magazine wall for the women's section.

My mind reeled with dreamy possibilities as I looked for the newest issue of NPBM! I saw Vogue and Bride and Allure Brides and thought 'the sky's the limit from here!'

When I located the NPBM issue I was again holding my breath with anticipation, flipping madly through the glossy pages while my heart was pounding in my chest and my eyes wildly scanning to find my published work!

I found it!
I found the gorgeously laid out full page spread! The layout showcased the bride's flowers and cake and there was a gorgeous shot of her and the groom that highlighted my work beautifully! Prominently placed on the page in color and a bold font was the full list of vendors and retailers responsible for putting this entire vision together.

I put my index finger on the column of vendors listed and ran it slowly down to find myself listed amongst the other talented vendors.

Venue? Check.
Dress? Check.
Bridal Shop? Check.
Florals? Check.
Tux? Check.
Jewelry? Check.
Rentals? Check.
Shoes? Check.
Wedding Planner? Check.

Cufflinks? Check.
Calligraphy? Check.
Invitations? Check.
Music and Entertainment? Check.
Beauty?
Beauty?
Beauty?

"Bueller….? Bueller…? Bueller…?"
-Econ Teacher, Ferris Bueller's Day Off

…my stomach sank and a large ball formed in the back of my throat. The hair and makeup was omitted. I had been omitted. There was zero mention of me or my salon. The shoes weren't even in any of the pictures featured and even THEY were mentioned?!!!?

How can this be when the NPBM staff themselves had emailed me? *They* contacted *me* to get my permission and confirm MY contact and booking information. I had been waiting for so long to see my work in print for the first time only to have the proverbial rug yanked out from underneath me.

How could this have happened? There must be a mistake, I'm just not seeing it. It has to be here, they said it would be here.

I felt numb.

My mind was reeling. I immediately pulled up the email info from the NPBM staff member that had contacted me originally about the feature all those months before. While still standing there in the magazine aisle of the Super Mart, I typed up a scathing email that was completely inappropriate. I deleted it without sending it. I typed up another version and deleted it as well. I then called the salon owner and with a shaky voice explained what had happened, or rather what had *not* happened.

When I got to the salon later that day she helped me put together a more appropriate version of the 'what in the actual fuckity-fuck happened' emails I had originally drafted. I sent it promptly and waited ... again.

A few days later I finally got a response. I'm of course paraphrasing because it's been years since this happened and I did not keep the original email but it went something like this...

Whoops!

Sorry about that! We'll put a correction in our online version soon.
We apologize for any inconvenience.
Best wishes,
NPBM team

Ummmm... thanks, I guess? You intend to put an 'oopsy-poopsy' fix online but not in your next print addition? Don't go too far out of your way there.

I then found myself obsessively checking their virtual magazine addition and website for the retraction/'oopsy-poopsy' fix. It was literally weeks. They had not fixed anything. I sent a follow up email and they finally responded in a lackadaisical fashion, sending the link for me to find the credit I was due.

I clicked the link and still had to dig four more pages deeper into their site to finally find a tiny black and white blurb that read, 'beauty services by Carleana Delacruz'. No picture of my work accompanying the blurb. No contact information for booking. No link back to the original feature. Nada.

It felt as though I was going from my name up in lights on Broadway, down to the personal ads buried in the back of the newspaper on page 42. Whaaaah. Whaaahh.

I wass equal parts validated and pissed. It was done. That was all that they were willing to give. The bright spot in my career at that point had been reduced to a tiny black and white blurb that even I had trouble finding while I was searching for it specifically. No potential bride or photographer was going to see my work and reach out to book my services based on this sad little blurb. But, it was over and I had to move forward.

The silver lining is that I could proudly say that my work had been published. Not just published but published in a household brand, nationally recognised publication. I knew the truth and I now know that I have to be my own advocate for all things. Today and everyday as a small business owner, I have to advocate for my credits and accomplishments and so do you.

Mind you, this is not an isolated incident. I have had countless times since this when I was scrolling the internet and randomly came across my work. I had no idea that a bride had submitted her wedding for publication or that a photographer had our project in print somewhere.

When I have found my uncredited work I have kindly and professionally messaged the entity that posted and let them know to add me and my contact info to the posting or whatever.

If the published work I found is in print and not online, clearly there isn't much anyone can do because the ship has already sailed. However, it certainly doesn't hurt to say something and stick up for yourself and your business.

Clearly the positives far outway the negatives when it comes to getting your work published or featured. Print gives a legitimacy to your body of work that is unparalleled. I've had a few hiccups along the way but all in all the good has outweighed the bad. Photographers and brides have found my work many, many times over to book Hairpins and Happiness for other events and collaborations.

Don't be discouraged by the hiccups. Make sure to triumph over them and relish in the fact that you will be recognised as a talented bridal stylist if you stick to it. Collaborate and submit your work often and with confidence. It will pay off. Promise.

Ask yourself...

- How many vendors have you reached out to prior to an upcoming booking?

- Do you stay to get BTS shots at bookings for social media posts?

- Will you contact a bride after the event to thank her? What will you say?

- Have you ever <u>not</u> asked for something (i.e. a job promotion, extra scoop of ice cream, etc...) and regretted it?

- Have you ever asked for something and regretted asking? (no matter what the outcome)

- Does the word 'no' instill fear in you? Why?

- Have you ever been let down by someone professionally?

- Have you felt that you have let someone else down professionally? What could you have done differently?

SET UP FOR SUCCESS

It's Your Stage and Your Rent is Due!

This chapter is a direct extension of the last. Professionalism isn't just looking and sounding good, it's also delivering on your promises!

We have all heard the cliche 'Under promise. Over deliver.'

It's a cliche for a reason. Cliches are often born out of truth. In business, especially the service industry, this couldn't ring more true.

A bride on her wedding day should feel well taken care of and pampered. Not stressed out about the timeline or quality of your work.

Long before the wedding day the bride should feel assured that you, as the beauty professional, will deliver on everything you promised her.

A big part of our job is to make sure that everyone involved has a clear understanding of what to expect from us, as the hairstylist and what we expect from them as the clients.

I start by having every bride fill out my inquiry form on my website. My calendar and everything is linked so that I can see right away if I'm available for their date, etc...

After they fill out the inquiry form I send them a more in

depth questionnaire. This covers things like the bridal party size, vibe, location, budget and a few other details. (sample of the questionnaire at www.hairpinsandhappiness.com) Making sure they're the right fit for me and my business as well as if I'm a good fit for them.

Once proposals have been sent, contracts have been signed and bridal previews (trials or practice updos) have been scheduled, there are still final details to tend to.

There should be an open line of communication in case anything needs to be adjusted. Getting ready locations change, a mom of the groom decides she *does* want her hair done after all, bridal portraits are being taken before the ceremony instead of after. The list of reasons goes on and on.

I don't include call times and end times on my contracts because this seems to be a very fickle business. I've had ceremony times shift, photographers tweak their timing and too many other variables to count.

* * *

Here are the 6 things you need to keep in mind and communicate to your brides to set yourself up for success at your next bookings…

1- Hair prep

Make sure there is clear communication about how the bridal party's hair should be prepped *before* you arrive on the day of the event.

Personally, I prefer clean, dry hair when doing up styles and formal work. (I'll 'dirty' it with my own products, thank you!) I want the bridal party's hair to be clean and dry so that I can cocktail what I need to achieve their desired look.

If there is something more specific that the bride needs to do for her desired look before my arrival, I make sure to inform her of those steps in advance.

Some of you may prefer a day dirty or even damp hair. Whatever your preference, make sure the bride *and* the bridal party are well aware of the expectations to make sure that you can keep a tidy timeline.

2- Figure out your timing.

Do not set yourself up for failure here. If you need more time, be honest with yourself before firming up the timeline with the bride/wedding planner. They all rely on you to give a realistic timeline and stick to it.

On average I take approximately 30 minutes per bridal service. (Yes, I move quickly and with purpose.) I plan on a full hour for the bride and I also tack on an extra 30 minutes at the end for touch ups and 'buffer' or wiggle room.

Example:
If the bridal party has 5 ladies total, including the bride, for hair only, I would book out 3 1/2 hours total. 1 hour for the bride + 2 hours for the four ladies + an additional 1/2 hour buffer = 3 1/2 hours.

3- Consider logistics.

Ask the bride (or wedding planner depending on the situation) a few simple questions before determining a start time. The answers to these next questions will help you determine the most ideal call time (start time).

-What time is the ceremony?
-When does the photographer arrive?
-Are you planning on a first look or any other photos before the ceremony?

-Is there any drive time between the getting ready location and ceremony venue?

After getting these answers you can make an educated timeline.

Example: Ceremony time = 2:00pm /Photographer arrival = 12:30pm /Yes to a first look/ Zero drive time, everything takes place at the same venue.

I would be comfortable with a 9:00am call time. When the photographer arrives at 12:30pm, I'll just be finishing touch ups and starting to do my clean up. (This also gives me a chance to introduce myself to the photographer, shake hands and exchange business cards etc.. we'll touch on this again later)

4- Comunicate

Make sure everyone is comfortable with the timeline.

After suggesting your start time to the bride/wedding planner they may want to tweak it.

"Can we start a bit earlier? I'd like a little extra time in the morning, just in case."

Those are things you can discuss, each situation is different.

If a bride has felt like the call time I've proposed is a little too early or late, I've certainly tweaked it. I'd hate for something as silly as a half hour to cause her any anxiety or fester uncertainty in my abilities to complete the task on time. But between you and I, I'm always ahead of the timeline because I'm aware of what I need to accomplish. I don't set myself up for failure. I do, however, set a sufficient and well appointed itinerary setting myself up for a successful wedding morning!

5- Schedule and day of timeline.

Personally, I do not suggest asking the bride/wedding planner for a specific list of who goes at what time. So long as there is a bum in my chair, I could care less if it's Becky's or Sally's bum. Ultimately, some brides will insist upon typing out a detailed itinerary... Becky starts at 7:30am and Debra will start at 8:05am and then Meg won't be there until 8:40am so she can go later...

None of this matters.

I always ask that the entire bridal party all arrive at the call time.

As I finish one person's hair I'll keep the flow going by asking who's ready to go next. I'm able to snag the next girl who's ready... if Becky was supposed to go first but slept in so she won't be here until whenever then we've already started our day behind schedule. Oftentimes the group will sit there idle waiting for Becky. This will set the entire day behind schedule.

Just don't allow it.

Never once have I ever followed a bride's itinerary to the letter. Not due to negligence mind you. Things happen.

I've had an insistent bride give me a detailed itinerary with the entire bridal party's names and exact whereabouts, down to the minute.

It makes the bride more comfortable to have it, so we have it. Expect Becky to be running late, Meg to have to go first and Karen to be running to the bathroom at the exact moment you're ready for her. It's the nature of the day. And that's okay.

If you as the beauty pro stand up and say with confidence, 'I can start whoever is ready!' They will fall in line. Any amount of time without a keister in your chair is wasted. Don't be rude. Be assertive. There is a difference.

6- Follow through

This is the secret sauce!

Although, I'm sure, it seems like a no brainer, you'd be amazed. Oh, the many things I've bore witness to...

For instance... I have been booked with additional makeup artists and stylists that have arrived over an hour late to their call time.

I once dealt with a severely hungover MUA that spent the entire morning tossing her cookies in the bridal suite's bathroom. Contrary to popular belief, the 'brown bottle flu' is not an acceptable excuse for mucking up your career. When she finally collected herself (ish) she promptly left and many of the bridal party were unable to get dolled up due to her immaturity and outrageous lack of professionalism.

Side note: It's a very uncomfortable situation when the bridal party is all whispering and eyes are darting back and forth across the room because of something so wildly negligent. Thank goodness this was not a situation where I had hired the extra set of hands. This was someone the bride had found on her own, that she knew outside of my recommendations. Otherwise, by proxy, I would look just as incompetent as her because I had recommended her. And Lawd knows I don't have time for those shenanigans!

I've heard stories about stylists canceling on their bookings at the last minute because a more lucrative opportunity came up.

These things are all *clearly* unacceptable. Gawd! I hope that's clear to the majority of my readers!

If you book a bride, you have committed to a high level of professionalism. Period.

If every Friday night is calling and you can't resist the urge to partake in drunkenness and tomfoolery; Do. Not. Book. The. Bridal. Party.

Prep- Timeline- Communicate- Logistics- Schedule-Follow Through

Now that we know the 6 simple things to set yourself up for success, things will run smoothly and you'll be able to wow your clients every time without so much as smudging your lipstick or breaking a sweat...

Questions to ask yourself:

- How can YOU help assure your brides that you'll deliver on your promises?

- Are you able to commit to all 6 steps?

- Are you relatable? Why?

- Do you have a bridal contract and questionnaire in place?

- What questions do you ask on your questionnaire?

- What would you do if someone showed up unable to perform their work?

The Stage:

"Success is never owned. It is rented and rent is due every day."
-Anonymouse

As a young, naive stylist fresh out of Cos School, I heard a phrase at a hair expo I attended that has stuck with me my entire career.

"Think of the salon floor as your stage."

All eyes are on you. You should always look and dress to impress when you're on the floor. Just as a dancer or actor would double check their makeup and hair before entering from stage left, you need to do the same when entering the salon floor. Wear the heels, rock the earrings, primp and prep like you're meeting your favorite celebrity. You are your own brand ambassador and CEO. You need to look and act the part.

This is for every client, every booking, every day, every shift.

I toured a salon once that had a sign up above the door going out from the break room to the styling floor that read 'Lights, Camera, ACTION!' I think of that often when walking out of my own break room onto the salon floor. I hold my head high and make sure my posture is on point. I smile and walk with confidence.

Just to be clear, I am not being fake. I have curated a positive attitude and am exuding confidence and a happy demeanor. We all have different versions of our real selves. We clearly don't act the same at a backyard bbq as we do at a plated, black tie gala. Don't be fake. Be the best you.

I guarantee you've never heard a friend say to someone, "If you're looking for a new hair girl, you just *have* to see my stylist! She always looks SO cozy!"

Don't be the flip-flop wearing, bad posture, slightly disheveled stylist. Be the well dressed, smiley, confident stylist.

You have no idea how often I have clients comment on what other salon staff are wearing and doing. Sometimes it's positive feedback, sometimes not. Believe me, there are always the usual suspects in every salon team.

"Why does he always look like he just woke up?"
"She's always so polished. I don't think I've ever seen her in jeans!"
"Wow, she always has the cutest shoes!"
"So, does she ever do her *own* hair or makeup?"
"Is she really wearing slippers to work?!"

This also translates into other character qualities ....

"She is always running behind, isn't she?"
"He seems to be really busy!"
"She's always in such a good mood! Is she singing, again?"

All I'm saying is, clients notice. Regular clients see the patterns. You don't want them to see the negative patterns in you. It does reflect on your business and the overall perceived value of their salon experience.

Although, within the salon we aren't trying to steal one another's clients, you may get a referral based on what they've seen. Or if a regular salon client can't get into their own stylist they may request you. This helps fill in those little gaps in your schedule until you're built up and booked solid. This also parlays into the bridal industry. More often than not, the client's regular stylist 'doesn't do weddings' and you end up with the booking for their events and special occasion hair largely due to the good impression you've already made on them.

Have you ever heard the saying, "Success is never owned; it's rented and rent is due every day"?

This is exactly what I'm talking about. We've all witnessed the 'salon queen' rise all the way to the top only to quickly fall from grace. She seemed to have it all. The money, the lifestyle, but then she lost her spark and quit 'paying the rent'.

She got too comfortable and started using the cruise control all too often. Arriving to work a little later. Dressing up a little less. Not doing the little extras for her clients. All those small things add up to big problems.

In order to thrive, you need to show up, be present, rock out your daily tasks, and dress the part. Head to toe.

Lights, Camera, Action!!

Your stage may be a salon floor one day, a meeting with a photographer at a coffee shop another day, and a church basement for an on-location wedding party the next. The same rules apply no matter what walls you're surrounded by. Look and act like a professional and you'll be perceived as a professional.

Pay your rent daily.

I know what some of you are thinking:

- "What if I can't afford the latest trends?"
- "You know, *some* people aren't *always* in a good mood."
- "I hate when people tell me how to dress and how to act."

If you don't walk the walk, the potential bride/client almost instantly loses faith in you and your abilities.

Fair or not, we are in the beauty industry. We aren't in the disheveled industry. We aren't in the half-assed-it-today industry. We certainly aren't in the ugly business. We own and operate a beauty business.

That being said, your style is your own and your brand is your own. If you appeal to a boho clientele and want to dress down a bit, go for it. You can style a pair of jeans to look put together and trendy with the right shoes and accessories. I'm not saying don't be yourself. You don't have to do anything you don't want to do. I'm saying put your best foot forward and look the part. Think of your brand from a client's perspective because their experience is and should always be, paramount.

I believe that everyone has a power outfit. One that they feel confident in. Close your eyes. Picture your closet. I'm going to describe two completely different daily agendas and you're going to picture your go-to outfit, right down to the shoes and hairstyle.

Scene one:
It's your day off. You sleep in later than usual because you don't have anything pressing to get done. You have a couple errands to do but nothing long or involved. Return recyclables and library books then pick up a handful of groceries. After running those errands you intend to head home and then go for a short bike ride instead of hitting the gym. It's a partly cloudy day at approximately 70'.

Do you have your outfit in your mind's eye? Good. Keep it out of your closet and hang it on a hook and we'll come back to it in a moment.

Scene two:
You can't sleep in today because you have a short but early day at your salon studio to meet with a potential bride, and then a lunch date with a photographer you've worked with in the past. After those quick meetings you intend to pick up a few salon essentials at your local supplier and then head home to cook dinner. The weather is partly sunny and about the same temperature as scene one.

Go pull that hypothetical outfit out of your closet.

Same outfit? Didn't think so.

For me, scene one is a pair of comfy burks or flip flops, dainty earrings, ripped warn-in jeans, a black tank or t-shirt and a messy bun on the top of my head topped with a pair of aviator sunnies as a headband. Minimal makeup; probably just a little mascara and tinted moisturizer.

On the other hand, scene two is going to start with a pair of trendy wedge sandals, a statement earring or necklace, either a black dress or a pair of dressy leggings and a tank paired with a fitted jacket that covers my bum and my hair pulled back into a polished low knot. I will be wearing all of the makeup that I would typically wear for a full day of work, including eyeliner, mascara, brow filler, tinted moisturizer and blush.

Try that outfit for scene two on in your mind. How's it feel? Are you standing a little taller? Making more eye contact? How's that posture?

Walking in to meet potential clients or other wedding vendors doesn't feel right in a pair of running shorts or a ponytail, does it? You also probably wouldn't swear at church sitting next to your grandma, but you may have a potty mouth at the bar with a group of old friends! It's not being untrue to yourself, it's knowing your audience. Professionalism is always going to get you further than not.

"You can never be overdressed or overeducated."

-Oscar Wilde

Your stage look isn't limited to how you dress and carry yourself physically.

Your brand is also reflected in your Marketing Funnel, which we'll dive into in the next chapter. For example, some introductions are made face to face with a firm handshake, while others are made via your internet presence or business cards.

Let's think past the color and font on your business cards and website. What else about your brand can you control that will provide an immersive experience into your aesthetic?

How does your business look? Feel? Smell? Sound?

Let's answer these questions using an example that we as hairstylists are all too familiar with; hairspray.

How does the packaging look and feel? Does it have a sleek, black label? Does it have a rubberized matte finish to the slender can? Feels bougie to the touch, doesn't it? And that lid clicks on just right. This can of hair magic smells of toasted vanilla and cedar wood, am I right? How much would you pay for this product? Would you expect to pay the same price at the SuperMart retailer for their store brand can of hairspray?

Let's compare the packaging to another hairspray... this one is in a square can. It has a unique shape and the label has a fun, youthful, multicolored design that happens to match the color of your bathroom towels! This one smells sweet and fruity like a favorite childhood candy. A lollipop mayhaps? The blue colored one?

Your client Andrea that loves a designer handbag and luxury products is going to love that black label. Your client Elizabeth that has a youthful vibe would be more likely to gravitate toward the multicolored candy label.

How does it smell? If either of these smelled like yesterday's sweat socks you probably wouldn't want your clients to make that purchase, correct? It could be the most amazing hairspray in the history of mankind, but I'm telling you right now, if it smells like the funky-bunch, nobody is buying that mamma-jamma!

Did you notice that I never once mentioned the *quality* of the actual product inside these cans? Here's why: in this chapter we're focusing on the full experience of your brand. You have to look expensive before you can be expensive. Yes, you need to be able to provide quality to your brides and their wedding parties, but first you need to have *perceived* value.

Here's a checklist to refer to when it's time to pay the rent:

- Hair on point
- Makeup done
- Smell good?
- Chic outfit
- Trendy shoes
- Positive Attitude
- Smile!

Check, check, checkity, check!!

To maintain rent-worthy status, keep these items on hand:

-Mirror (after lunch, check your teeth. Quick check for makeup smudges, etc...)
-Deodorant (for reapplying when needed)
-Makeup essentials (i.e. lipstick/chapstick, powder, oil papers... pick your poison)
-Mints or mouthwash (duh)
-Tooth picks or floss (again, duh.)
-Tylenol/Asprin or the like (a head-achey stylist is a grumpy stylist)
-Cute back up shoes (in case the super cute heels can't make it through a full shift)
-Protein packed snacks (because if you're like me, you don't wanna be hangry mid shift!)

-Perfume or fragrance (don't overdo it)
-Phone charger
-Lint roller
-Nail file/nail glue (things happen and you don't want to catch a client's hair with a snaggle nail)

Things to ponder:

- What do brands that appeal to you, do to attract you as a customer?

- What does your salon space smell like? Why?

- What do your clients hear when they meet you? Music? What genre?

- What's your favorite hairspray? Why?

- What is your current power outfit?

- Do you speak differently in front of your peers versus your boss? How so?

MARKETING FUNNEL:

Why It's So Important and How
to Build One that Works

Here we are, the infamous Marketing Funnel chapter. First comes professionalism, then comes your Marketing Funnel. Why is it second and not first? Because everything you do as a bridal beauty expert, including your funnel, will ring with professionalism when done correctly!

In the not too distant past, stylists didn't have social media to help us be found. We had to solely rely on regular clients and face-to-face professional relationships for potential brides to find us. Luckily for us, that has all changed and we now have free marketing available to us 24/7. Welcome to the stage, internet and social media!

I'm aware that this isn't earth shattering news. However, it's often overlooked and seems overwhelming. Therefore, it's not done well, or worse, not done at all.

Not an option. You need to establish an online presence. You need a Marketing Funnel.

A Marketing Funnel describes your prospective customer's journey with you from beginning to end. From initially learning about you and your business, to booking, then purchasing. The whole kit and Caboodles*!

I'm not tech savvy. I repeat: I am NOT tech savvy. What I know are things I've learned through trial and error. I hope to help your journey be a little less frustrating if you aren't tech-y like me. I only know how to do what I know how to do, so bear with me. Also, keep in mind, this is not evergreen* material. The nature of social media is fickle at best and updates are always happening, so what's here may be more brown than green. Nonetheless, this is where we are currently, and the core of this information is imperative.

If you get overwhelmed, remember - "piano, piano..."

In today's world we are all aware that we need to have an online presence. We need to be searchable on the web. It's an absolute necessity.

My first introduction to the concept of a Marketing Funnel was from Britt Seva, salon education extraordinaire, and creator of the *Thriving Stylist* brand. Her concept is a bit more in depth and actually teaches to a marketing hourglass rather than a funnel, so if that piques your interest, you should check her out. Many business gurus within the beauty industry and beyond teach the Marketing Funnel. They all do this because it works.

Look what I made! It's a Marketing Funnel!

Awareness
Drive traffic to your website

Interest
Engage with your new audience

Desire
Entice consumer to want the looks you advertise

Trust
Convince consumer to purchase with you

Purchase
$$$

Basically, a Marketing Funnel takes a potential consumer becoming aware of you, then yada (interest), yada (desire) yada (trust), then turning it into profit. Profit, otherwise known as money, can be a booking, service or a purchase of goods. Or, more simply put, your Marketing Funnel catches the vague consumer and helps nurture that consumer into a loyal, sales producing customer.

Awareness is the first step. You have to catch those little search nuggets and nurture them into thriving purchases. This starts with things as simple as handing out your business cards, using hashtags in your posts, and networking with other industry professionals. In this first phase of your Marketing Funnel, you're introducing yourself as a professional, whether it be in person, or in an online social forum like Instagram, Pinterest, TikTok, Facebook, or whatever else comes along. Now people know who you are! Next you need to show them what you do.

Interest is where we start the nurturing process. Now that the potential client has heard of you, interaction needs to follow. Do this by being present on social media. It doesn't have to be excessive, but your presence needs to help them understand and get excited about your brand, vibe, and ability. A clean and professional social media presence will help do just that.

Desire "Ooh, look at that pretty bride, I want to be her! I must hire this stylist so that I can be as sparkly and pretty as her!" People aspire to be the people living their best lives on social media. You can make that dream come true for them.

Trust is proving that you as the stylist are capable of reproducing the looks advertised via your social media and website. Think behind the scenes photos, captions, and hashtags.

Referrals from other professional wedding vendors help to legitimize your brand. Sharing your published and featured work from collaborations with photographers, wedding planners and gown designers also prove you can do what you claim.

If the first few steps are in place, and your website has the same vibe and messaging, you're set up to receive inquiries to motivate sales.

Purchase is the final step of the marketing funnel. This conversion takes place when we have built our professional relationship with the consumer throughout the entire funnel. Awareness, interest, desire, and trust have led to loyalty and purchases. That is when sales are made. Dollar Dollar Bills, Ya'll!

The funnel only works to its full potential when all of the steps are fully functioning. Skip the social media? Your funnel is broken. Don't bother with a website? Stop breaking your funnel!!

How will you know if your funnel is functioning properly? Simply, you'll know because you will have consistent inquiries from *solid* leads that you *want* to work with!!

Popularity or Profitability?

In today's world it's human nature to get caught up in the social media game. Please keep in mind that your goals should always be profitable over popular. Don't get sidetracked by the number of followers or likes you have or don't have on any social media platform. It is meant to be a tool to show off your best work. Keeping up with the Jones' can be a slippery slope. Just don't go there. The likes and followers that you do have need to be profit oriented. Buying followers is an inflated ego boost that isn't profitable. Who cares how many followers you have? Your bank account? Nope. Your vacation fund? Nope. Why do we get caught in that hamster wheel? Think profitable when you post. Popularity doesn't pay the bills, just ask all the 'IT' girls from your high school. Are the prom queens making any money based off of their pubescent popularity efforts? Probably not. Lets not peak too early by worrying about how popular we are. Let's instead be sure to post scalable, profitable material that shows our potential clients how professional and awesome our businesses really are! Popularity be damned.

Choose a username or handle that reflects what you do!

"@himynameistori1" may be understandable to you, Tori, but that generic username isn't going to let anyone know what you do if they come across you in their social media feed.

Now, this is a complex issue. There are plenty of arguments to keep your current username, especially if you already have a strong following or you already have a lot of professional vendors that tag you often.

If you change your username, they likely won't take the time to follow your new name right away or won't realize you have a new name. Risky.

If instead you choose "@torithehairstylist1" as your handle, users would know what you do, but nothing specific about your talents and location.

I went through this while building my business. Starting from scratch and reestablishing a username is scary. It is a slow build because you want it to be organic so that your followers are actually engaging with your posts.

Buying followers is not as helpful as one might hope. You will ultimately be spending your money on bots and disengaged users, not authentic followers. Although you may feel like it looks impressive to have the 10k flag at the top of your profile, if they're robots then they aren't potential customers. If they aren't potential customers then they are not going to spend money with you or share your work with other potential customers. See my point?

Write a Bio that's specific

In your Bio section there is room to give further description of your specific skill set. Remember to be short and to the point because there are a limited amount of characters permitted in these sections. Abbreviations and emojis are your friends here! For example, "MI" instead of "Michigan," or a lipstick emoji instead of "makeup artist."

Currently these sections are 'key word' sensitive, meaning if someone searches for 'stylist' and your profile uses that word, your page will be in the heap of profiles that pop up.

Ideally, you should also include a 'call to action' like "click here," or "inquire below,"or "drop me a message," at the link you provide.

Your Instagram profile may look something like this:

@torithehairstylist1
Tori | Bridal Specialist
Beauty Salon
Hello my name is Tori!
Here to beautify the modern bride!
MI based on location-hair & makeup (lipstick emoji) **
#torithehairstylist1
All Inquiries visit...
www.torithehairstylist1.com

Curate your portfolio

Your online presence is meant to act as a portfolio of your work. Every picture on your website and social media will both showcase your abilities and ideal clients.

Photos

What are photos? Photos are literally pictures taken of your best, most brag-worthy, work.

If you don't have any professional photos* of your work, you can take your own in the meantime. The photos of your work should be crisp and well-lit. Make sure to take those photos near a natural light source (facing a window is best) and against a clean background, so as not to distract from the detail of your work.

You want to be sharing and posting more of the things you want to be doing. Take photos that highlight your interests and talents. If you dislike boho braids, for the love of gawd don't share a ton of photos of boho braids! If instead you love a sleek french twist or classic low knot please, please, PLEASE show us more of that!!

Clean, not sterile. Show your personality without looking cluttered or too personal. (We don't need any photos from young Billy's little league game in the background. Although it would be a personal touch, it wouldn't look professional. It's a fine line that we have to walk.) Use your best judgment. When in doubt, visit some of the websites and social media pages that you look up to and often draw inspiration from. I can almost guarantee that they are uncluttered, clean masterpieces.

*See Chapter 7, Booking Shoots

Captions

What are captions? A caption is a description of the photo or post. Captions can include text, hashtags, @ mentions and emojis.

Captions are ideally meant to entertain or educate. Ask a question to get users involved with your post. Provoke thought, guidance or humor.

Posting something along the lines of 'loving this summer blonde' isn't thought provoking. It's actually quite redundant. This is frankly, a work in progress for me. I recognize that I need to do better. I've come a long way.

Hashtags

What are hashtags? Hashtags are a combination of words, numbers or emojis following the # symbol. They are used in social media to make your content more discoverable.

There is a bit of controversy among social media gurus as to whether or not we should wipe our socials clean of all the poorly lit and less than fantastic posts from yesteryear. I have chosen to keep mine as a sort of timeline. #thenandnow if you will.

Using a hashtag like #bride will technically put your post among a lot of people searching #bride (84.8 million posts last I checked) Being the devil's advocate, that also means that thousands of posts are tagged with that same hashtag daily and therefore bump yours down the list, making it less visible and less relevant, unless someone's doing a really deep dive.

Using a hashtag that's more specific like #bridalhair brings the posts down to 6.6 million, and even the more specific #michiganbridalhair is down to just over one thousand posts, keeping you at the top of the heap. We want to be a bigger fish in a smaller pond whenever possible, right?

Depending on the project, I like to use a medley of broad and specific hashtags.

Broad spectrum hashtags = tags like #bride #hair & #stylist
Specific hashtags = #eastlansingbride #midwestweddinghair & #michiganhairstylist

I make sure to use #hairpinsandhappiness to tag all of my work. That hashtag is so specific that you'll only find it if you are familiar with me and my work. That means if you do search it, you'll immediately find a gallery of my work! This has worked for me time and time again.

A common question is "How many hashtags should be used in a single post?" This, again, is not evergreen. In the spring of 2023, most influencers are suggesting an optimal 15 - 30 hashtags on a single post. This is debatable of course and if you were to ask 10 different influencers the same question on Monday they will all likely have a different answer for you by Wednesday.

Tagging

Tagging is different from hashtagging.

When you're tagging another influencer or wedding vendor you're literally adding their @username in the comment section of a post. When tagging a place you're literally adding the geographical location to a post. Tagging accomplishes two things.

1- It alerts the 'taggy' to show them you have shared something on your feed to help promote their work as well. (Love fest ensues and all the sharing, commenting and tagging that you can handle will undoubtedly come to fruition!)

2- Makes your feed more visible to other users that follow those @usernames and/or geographical locations.

Website

What is a website? A website is a collection of web pages linked together and found on the World Wide Web using a domain name. The purpose of your website is to show your work and give information about your business.

When creating your website you can keep it simple. Start small. You can always add to it later. Make sure it's straightforward and easy to navigate.

I used Wix to build and host my website. I found it to be user friendly and easy to use. I know of other stylists that use sites like WordPress, Weebly, and GoDaddy to build their websites and they seem happy with the outcome.

It is imperative that you have a website. If you skip this important step in your Marketing Funnel, the funnel is broken.

Some stylists skip this step thinking that using Facebook or Instagram as their main online representation is adequate. This may be true for the short term, but what about the long term? What if your social media of choice loses its popularity? Remember MySpace? It was the mecca of social media at one point and is now rendered almost completely obsolete. Building a website that you own and operate ensures its longevity.

Keep the overall look as in sync with your branding as possible. Fonts and color schemes should reflect your social media and business cards. Take a step back from your new creation and look at it as a consumer. Ask trusted people in your life to take a look at it and be open to feedback. It doesn't have to be perfect to launch it. You can go back and tweak it as you collect more images, decide on different verbiage or change your prices. Potential clients should feel like they already recognize the site upon their very first visit. It's a reflection of your work and your other Marketing Funnel components that they've already been privy to.

Now that your site is built you'll need a host. For uniformity and simplicity, I use Wix for a small monthly fee. It is an automatic sum removed from my business account so it never even crosses my mind. Currently, I pay less than $100 annually.*

* Wix is not a sponsor of this book, I just really like them and their product.

Make sure that your business name is available in the ".com" world. Use a site like GoDaddy.com to find a domain name that's available, suits your business, and can be readily found in a Google search.

You'll want a ".com" rather than a ".org" or a ".net" (good luck getting a .gov) When it comes to internet browsing, ".com" is king! Using alternatives can negatively impact the way consumers can find you.

Choosing a domain name that reflects your business type or name is important so that you're easily found on the world wide web. If you choose something too difficult to pronounce or spell it's nearly impossible to find in the sea of other options.

Catchy AND memorable is best.

This is exactly why I opted not to use my actual name, but instead a small phrase that I feel depicts what I do and how I feel about my profession. CarleanaDeLaCruzHairStylist.com is too heavy in vowels and pronunciation possibilities! Believe me, I've heard them all!

CarLENa? CarlEEna? Carelina? CarOlina? CarleeANNA? CarMELLa? Catrina? CoraLin? Karina? KEErlina? CoraLINEa? Carla? Darlene?

DEElaCruz? DILLa Cruz? PelaCruz? DayLaCruze? DeeLeeCruz? DeliCruise? DelAcuRz? DellacUrz? DelAcres? Delalvuz? DelaCruzz?

And let's not even get started on my very Italian maiden name of Garagiola!

Although my name is unique and you'd be hard-pressed to find another bridal hair stylist with the same spelling of Carleana DeLaCruz out there, I thought it better to keep things simple for my website.

This is true on the other side of the coin as well; if your name is extremely common it will prove to be just as difficult for potential clients to find and book the correct Jennifer Jones or Katie Smith! (Sorry ladies!)

Also, let's think ahead a bit: if you are currently single and your entire brand is built around your maiden name, what will you do if you end up getting married and want to change your last name? If a name change is in the realm of possibilities, you may want to avoid using your current last name. It's obviously up to you and you can certainly change or keep your business name no matter what your future holds, just give it some thought.

Hairpins and Happiness reflects what I do and how I feel, as well as how I want my clients to feel. Happiness is often in short supply these days; let's spread joy whenever we can! I felt that the name Hairpins and Happiness was cheeky but not corny or overly sales-y.

Let me ask you a couple questions:

- Do you have a precise business name?
- Are you searchable on Google?
- Is your domain name memorable and easy to spell?
- Do you have social media profiles set up?

It's easy to get caught up in the creative process and not let your new baby , errr... website, out into the world. It can be scary actually. Set those fears aside and let it out into the world. That little baby bird has to leave the nest or all your time and efforts were for nothing.

Don't get to the finish line and trip right before you cross it.

Do the damn thing, even if it's a scary thing.

Remember you are your brand. Your brand should be obvious and cohesive throughout your funnel. Think beyond fonts and colors. Be you. Be relatable. Be real.

"If you aren't relatable, you aren't bookable." - Me (AKA: CarLEEna DeliCruise)

Back to our funnel...

I am here to give you the elevator pitch. The shorthand version that worked for me. I built 99% of my website myself. Started with one site builder, found a different one that I was more comfortable with and through trial and error did the thing.

(With a little help from a tech wizard friend or two! Thanks Chris and Co!)

Wix is essentially a 'drag and drop' program that I was able to navigate more easily than others I had messed with prior. It has basic layouts and prompts that you can embellish by changing the colors and fonts to suit your aesthetic. Drop a few images of you and your work and you're well on your way!

This portion of the program can get overwhelming and feel impossible. Again, If **I** can, **you** can!

Take a break. Take a step back. Ask a friend or coworker what they think about the site. Keep it simple. You can always come back to make changes and updates later.

You don't need to build perfection. What you need to build is function.

It's easy to get caught up in the minute details of a site and 'hem and haw' over the perfect color for the background or which font to use for this or that. Try to stay focused on the objective. You need a functional site to run your beauty business. Once you have your basics in place, you've spell checked and she's got her lipstick on and ready for the prom; put it out there and publish the site. It's not doing you or your business any good stalled out on your computer.

I repeat. Publish the website. Get it live! As soon as potential clients can find you via your marketing funnel and contact you through your website, you are doing the thing! You are up and running and I guarantee it will feel amazing and empowering.

❄ ❄ ❄

Let's make something very clear. I am not 'techy' by any stretch of the imagination. Ask anyone who knows me, and they will readily confirm.

So when I say If I can do it, you can do it. I mean just that.

* * *

Note: If you take nothing else from this book, I hope you take this- without an effective and functioning Marketing Funnel, potential clients will look elsewhere for their bookings. This, I promise.

Let's sum things up a bit: All things in the awareness portion of the funnel should lead to your socials and in your profile and bio on your socials there should be a clear link to your website. Once they reach your website they should have an easy to find inquiry form. After the inquiry has been submitted, because they have been wooed by your beautiful website, you fire back a questionnaire and from there the ball is in your court! Boom! Mic drop.

Things to Consider:

- Do you already have a marketing funnel in place?
- If so, is it functioning correctly?
- What part of your funnel needs some attention?
- Socials in place?
- Website up and running?
- Are you relatable? Why?
- Do all your online platforms mesh and have the same vibe?
- Is your branding clear on all socials and follow through to

your website?

- Are you a popular prom queen or a profitable CEO?

BOOKING PHOTO SHOOTS

No Buts, Just Do The Thing!

At every wedding, there is a photographer.

It is wildly important to build relationships with photographers. It is because of their amazing art that your amazing art looks so amazing! Are you picking up what I'm laying down here?

"But how do I build relationships with people that I don't even know and haven't even met?"

Simple.

As i mentioned earlier, before you show up for a booking, always ask the bride or wedding planner who the vendors are that you'll be working with. This way you can search their social media and follow them ahead of time as a professional courtesy. This also makes it easier to find your work later on when they post pictures of the event.

Being a veteran stylist, I often find out that I'm going to be working with some of the usual suspects. I know their work and I know that the day will be smooth sailing if my local faves, All Grande Events or EYP Weddings are involved. I also know that they do an amazing job of suggesting talented teams of wedding vendors, including photographers and videographers. My job is easier because of their professionalism.

Other times there isn't a planning team involved, but nevertheless I'm somewhat familiar with the photographer or venue because I've already worked with them in the past. That is a luxury that comes with time and dedication. If I'm unfamiliar with them, I *get* familiar with them via social media and their websites.

Once you have scoured their social media, feel free to reach out via private message with a simple "Looking forward to working with you on 8/27/25 at Jane and John's wedding!"

This tells them that you're active on socials and that you're interested in furthering a professional relationship.

Note: It is extremely rare that a wedding vendor does not reciprocate your olive branch.
They want exposure just as much as you do. Like. Follow. Comment. Always.

Remember your Marketing Funnel - you want your Instagram (and other socials) to reflect professionalism and act as a portfolio of your work. In order to book more work you need professional photos. You get professional photos by booking more work.

When I was first starting out in the freelance bridal industry I often 'cold called' wedding vendors.

Okay, I didn't literally *call* them. Nobody's answered a phone since 1999. I would message them. Start with a compliment, introduce yourself, offer to collaborate on future projects.

One of the results of these new relationships may be that you're asked to participate in a stylized photo shoot. Sometimes these shoots act as professional courtesies to the other vendors involved. Everyone scratches one another's backs in order to gain beautiful images that everyone can use for their websites and marketing materials.

Please know that there is generally no money exchange for these efforts. You're paid with experience, exposure, and the coveted photos from the collaboration. This falls under the umbrella of 'you have to give first before you get'. The paid gigs will fall in line after you have some experience with the pro-courtesy shoots under your belt.

I still do a lot of pro-courtesy styled shoots because I genuinely enjoy creating. These environments give me a chance to get out of the "office" and flex my creative muscles. The knowledge that you helped bring a creative vision to life is unparalleled.

Sometimes the photos are submitted for publication, and very often they parlay into another paid gig down the road. This industry is all about relationships. Build professional relationships with your fellow wedding vendors and they'll suggest you for future bookings. And that my friends, is where the money is made. Trust the process.

Eventually, after you've built a good reputation for yourself amongst these other wedding vendors, the work just starts to flow in! It's effortless! Now you can just kick back and watch the inquiries roll in!

Just kidding.

Rent is due, remember?

I can almost hear some of you asking "But, what if I don't want to wait to be asked to collaborate for a stylized shoot?"

My answer is to leave those What-If-Monsters in your dust and make it work. Get the images.

"Talent is a pursued interest.
Anything that you're willing to practice, you can do."
-Bob Ross

We all have a camera in our back pocket these days. If you've reached out to every photographer or human with a camera that you can think of and aren't getting anywhere in the timeline you've determined for yourself, that's okay.

Grab a friend, client, colleague, family member, or anyone with hair and start playing around with it. Get a couple snaps on your phone in natural lighting with a plain background. Clean looks that are brightly lit always translate best to photos.

A simple background is a must. Do not reinvent the wheel here. You're trying to show off your work. Any clutter, busy prints, or garden landscapes behind your work can be extremely distracting.

Brighten up the snaps you've taken on your phone in an editor app, but not too much. You want them to look clean, not washed out. I have tried different apps over the years, and they're all pretty interchangeable other than a few bells and whistles. Find the one that works best for you.

After doing a few DIY shoots, you can level up easily! You can start by asking photography students at your local community college if they're interested in collaborating. Ask those same friends with hair to model for you again. Reach out to local bridal shops and ask to borrow sample gowns in exchange for sharing the photos with them. They may appreciate the exposure, and they can use them to promote their own business.

You can get beautiful images of your work for little to zero money. You just need to get creative.

Now that you have some semi-professional photos to use, you'll have your sea legs and you'll have an increased confidence for future collaborations and bookings.

I know this process well, because the first few shoots beyond what I took with my own camera were initiated by me. I knew a friend of a friend that was taking some photography classes at our local community college. I reached out to them and grabbed a couple of family friends, aka 'models'. We shot at a studio space that the professor of the student photographer allowed students to use outside of class.

We got some really great images out of the project! Nothing groundbreaking, but they were a solid start!

I felt accomplished because I had professional grade photos to start using for my professional portfolio, social media, and website. I had taken control of my fate.

No more What-If-Monsters. Do the thing, even if it's scary.

Ponder Worthy Questions:

- Have you ever reached out to mutual vendors before a booking?

- Who can you contact to ask if they're interested in photographing your work?

- Who will you ask to be your hair model?

- Are you already mentally plotting out your next shoot?

- What inspires you professionally?

BRIDAL PREVIEWS:

Trials, Practices and Previews. Oh, My!!

Whether we call it a bridal preview, trial, or practice, we all know what we're talking about. The test-run to ensure that the bride loves her look on the day of her wedding.

I don't always do a test run, it depends on what the bride wants and needs. These days, there are two kinds of brides: the ones who insist on a practice run of their entire bridal look, and the ones that would rather send a few inspiration photos and forgo that step altogether. Let's put a hairpin in that bride that doesn't need the whole shebang for now. We'll start with the one that wants the in-person experience.

Over the years, some of my brides have wanted me to replicate the <u>exact</u> photo they found in a magazine or on Pintrest or TikTok. They want to make sure it lasts all day and night, and have the full experience to confirm that look works for them.

Others want to see a few different options. They may want to add a braid, see it with a few more pieces down to frame the face, see the bun higher or lower, you get it. They also generally want to take photos of each look, and maybe even ask multiple friends and family for their opinions. Trying multiple looks doesn't mean they didn't like your original work. It often means they didn't feel like themselves, or they wanted to see more options, or they'd like it a little more off the face to show off grandma's earrings that they intend to wear. More on grandma's earrings later in this chapter.

All brides have different comfort levels with the entire wedding planning process. Hair and makeup isn't any different; it's another decision they have to make. Some brides are indecisive and others are more decisive. Neither process is right or wrong.

The indecisive bride always has a lot of questions: "Would this look good on me?" "What do you think would look best?" "Do you think I should have a side or center part?" "Why do you think that?" "What are other brides doing with their hair right now?" "Have you been doing a lot of high buns this wedding season?" "Do you think I can pull this look off?"

The decisive bride needs very little reassurance and knows what she's comfortable with and what looks right on her for her sense of style.

Both indecisive and decisive brides offer their own challenges and rewards. Embrace them and enter every bridal preview appointment with confidence. You've got this.

I make sure to set aside a full hour to an hour and a half for my bridal previews. I rarely use the entirety of the appointment, but I want to make sure that she feels that all of her questions have been answered and that she feels at ease about her day of wedding look.

I start every bridal trial by going over the 'cliff notes' of the contract. Firming up call times and end times, venue address, total number of ladies getting hair and makeup services, and so on. For example, I remind the bride that everyone needs to come with clean, dry hair. Although this is in the fine print of my bridal contracts this is a great time to remind the bride to pass that info onto her bridal party. It's important that you finalize these things closer to the actual wedding date, because at that point, there are so many vendors involved it can be hard for the bride to remember who she told what.

Once we've firmed everything up, we get to the fun stuff. We start looking at inspiration photos and talking about what the dress and accessories look like.

I suggest the bride look for inspo photos of similar hair colors. (Length isn't as tricky anymore now that we have so many options for extensions and wefting available.) The same exact up style looks different on a brunette, redhead and blonde. They could have the same length and texture but blondes show more dimension than someone with darker tones. It just is what it is. If a brunette wants more dimension in their up style you may want to talk to them about some soft highlights to create the depth they're wanting. This is all a part of the bridal preview process.

Instagram, Pintrist, WeddingWire, bridal magazines etc... are all great places to look for wedding hair inspo. I tell my brides to take a screenshot and save to a private board or album to share with me later.

Speaking of which: Make sure that she knows to bring any and all options for jewelry and veil. Anything that may adorn her hair on the day of should be brought as well. Fresh flowers, tiaras, sparkly bits, veils and the like!

If they have a veil that is a long cathedral length or is multi-tiered and full, you may want to suggest they don't bring it to the bridal preview. Since I perform the preview at my salon, you never know what random splatters of hair color or product may be lurking around in case that gorgeous swath of fabric hits the floor. I have been known to hold up a tissue to show where the veil would fall on the head instead of risking an unsightly stain on the bride's veil. This is a creative substitution when you're in a pinch and forced to improvise!

I once had a bride bring in a treasure trove full of her grandma's jewelry to her bridal preview. Amongst the stately collection there were brooches, hairpins, large pendants, and earrings. Through tears and wistful smiles I helped the bride, sister, and mother choose which pieces were going to adorn their hair on the day of the wedding.

Her grandmother must have been quite the lady! These pieces were very unique and reflected a champagne taste on a champagne budget! The top choice for the bride was an antique hair comb with natural freshwater pearls twisted onto fine gold wiring. The elegance of the heirloom was reflected in the lack of patina and was easily bent to enhance her final look. It was the perfect nod to a lost loved one and beautifully embellished her lightly textured low bundle of curls.

Another example of a bride using a unique embellishment was that of a small elephant charm.

It was a gift to the bride from her mother-in-law-to-be from one of her exotic trips. Some cultures believe the elephant symbolizes strength, loyalty, and spiritual well-being. Some others believe that they symbolize happiness and good fortune. Whatever the case here, this bride wanted to incorporate the little gold fella into her upstyle. I was happy to weave a bit of neutral colored string through the tiny hole in the top of the charm to literally sew it into the bride's hair. I always keep some 'hair colored' string and a plastic craft needle in my kit for just such an occasion. You can never be too prepared.

Although the elephant wasn't a traditional heirloom piece, it may be one day. We really do play an important role in incorporating all of these tiny details on the most important day of someone's life. I'm constantly reminded of how personal and sentimental our career can be. We play a role in the biggest day of people's lives and that is beyond humbling. I don't take it for granted and neither should you.

"Happiness and confidence are the prettiest things you can wear on your wedding day."
-Taylor Swift

Ultimately, our job as the hair stylist or makeup artist is to enhance the brides' natural beauty so that they feel like the most confident, beautiful version of themselves on their wedding day.

By the completion of the bridal preview the bride should be smiling ear to ear. She has yet another thing checked off her long list of wedding to-do's. She knows that you're a confident and capable stylist. She has a clear visual of what she will look like on the biggest day of her life and she is radiating happiness.

All is good.

Some potential clients want to test you out *before* booking or paying a deposit. This doesn't happen often but every once in a while I'll have a request for one.

I'm honestly torn by this scenario. Half of me thinks with confidence, okay, so we do the preview now instead of later - we both know she's booking. The other half thinks, nah. We needn't waste one another's time. Book now, preview later. In my experience, oftentimes when brides want to test drive before buying they are price shopping. They also tend to require a lot more attention in the form of back and forth about what-if Bridesmaid Becky doesn't want makeup now but wants an updo instead of a braid... ain't nobody got time for that. It's a personality type that needs an abundance of reassurance and handholding via emails and text.

By agreeing to the test drive before booking, you run the risk of losing that coveted date from any other brides that may want to book you sight unseen. If they opt out, you're left with nothing.

You, as the professional, need to work out what's best for you and your business.

Now, let's address the bride that doesn't need the test-run that we put a hairpin in earlier.

Long ago, every bride came into the salon for a 'practice updo,' then came back with her entire bridal entourage on the day of the wedding. Due to the magic of technology and how brides find us these days, our industry and the nature of bridal bookings has changed significantly.

Logistics alone will prevent some brides from requesting a bridal preview. If my bride in Florida or Kansas can't make it to the Mitten-State for a trial run then that's just fine. We can always video chat via FaceTime or Skype to talk about what she wants done with her hair. She can also email or text me inspiration photos so that I can make sure I'm well prepared for the day of the wedding. In these circumstances, still remember to confirm all the details via email or phone that you would have covered in your in-person bridal preview.

No matter if your bridal preview is in person or not, you now have the tools to make your bride feel at ease and confident in your abilities. And don't forget, your bride will be comfortable and excited about your work and professionalism due to your marketing funnel being ammmaaaazing.

You got this.

Things to ask yourself:

- How much time do you book a Bridal Preview appointment for?

- What questions do you ask the bride at the preview appointment?

- How do you tell a bride to prepare for the bridal preview?

- How do you tell a bride to prepare for the wedding day? Is there a difference?

- What's the most unique thing you've ever heard of adorning a bride's hair??

- Do you allow trials/previews before the date is booked and/ or a deposit has been made?

CONTRACTS AND PRICING:

The Tale of the Peasant Stylist

Now that we have our marketing funnel, social media, referrals, and all the website amazingness, what's next?

Your pricing structure. It's not a sexy topic but we have to tackle it.

Things look a bit different on the booking and pricing front from when I first started out doing bridal hair two decades ago. I literally received all my wedding bookings through the front desk at the commission-based salon I was employed at the time.

Let's travel back in time here... close your eyes... err hypothetically at least...

Imagine a petite little ol' grandma telling you the following story with her wise, weathered voice, while wearing a sensible, matching cardigan set and clutching her small basket purse...

"Picture it,

a small village, called East Lansing, Michigan ,

2003. There was a beautiful Peasant Stylist, fresh

out of cosmetology school, awaiting her fate.

She sat in the break room with the other stylists, day

after day, waiting for the busy-bus to drop off more walk-

in clients. No internet, just a small screen on a flip phone

without a camera. The stylists had to make conversation

or stare at the wall to pass the time. When the front desk told the Peasant Stylist she had a wedding party, they also informed her of the pay she'd receive upon the split with the salon. They booked it for the Peasant Stylist by chiseling the information into a stone tablet otherwise known as a pencil and a paper scheduling calendar.

At the time of the practice updo, the bride would bring in distorted, poorly printed images from the world wide web or torn pages from bridal magazines. On the rare occasion that the hair was to be done on location instead of in the salon, the bride would bring home-printed directions to the venue (one way) from MapQuest.*

The Peasant Stylist hoped that everyone that signed up for hair services still wanted it done, for if not, then she didn't get compensation for the last minute cancellation. After completing everyone's hair, the Peasant Stylist would have to stand around awkwardly awaiting payment from each individual bridesmaid before she could depart, for this was the first exchange of money. She was to be paid by cash, check, or doubloons.. In those days it was impossible to accept any plastic currency without a landline and large credit card machine outside of a brick and mortar business.

The Peasant Stylist would then have to follow the MapQuest* directions backwards (turning left when it says right and right when it says left) to make her long journey back to the salon where she would then split her meager earnings with the Mafiosi, err... salon owners, 50/50. That was business.

That young Peasant Stylist was me...

and that story is true."

"Travel down the road and back again"
-Golden Girls Theme Song

This is not an exaggeration. This is how the first few years of my bridal beauty journey started. Good thing I'm not directionally challenged and that I was able to keep my mind open to technological updates and industry changes along the way. I'm not going to lie, some tech developments I sought out and some I stumbled upon by happenstance. I've come a long way, baby!

*For those of you born after the year 2000, who *haven't* already Googled 'MapQuest' please see 'Lingo' later in the book for a brief definition. I pray history doesn't repeat itself.

Thinking back over my career alone, I have witnessed bridal norms change drastically! Some things have changed due to technology, others because of fashion shifts.

When a bride came into the salon for a trial updo 15 or 20 years ago, she brought tangible, printed pictures of what she wanted. These pictures were either torn from a bridal magazine or printed at home. The at-home print was generally done with a low ink cartridge so the coloring was all faded and funky and there were thick, horizontal stripes going through the photo. But if you squinted you could see the detail! Kinda... a little... ehh... not really.

Now brides come into the salon with an arsenal of inspiration photos they've pinned or saved from sites like Pinterest, Wedding Wire and Instagram. It's not any better or worse, just different. At the time I had thought nothing of the shabbily home printed photos of the past, that's all we had. As a matter of fact, if they came with a picture *at all* back in the early 2000's they were over achievers! Currently, they typically come to my salon studio for their bridal preview and we go over their mood boards and inspiration photos on a smartphone or tablet while firming up details for their event.

Now that we are speeding twenty years forward from the Peasant Stylist scenario, things look completely different.

Now, my clients find my business via my Marketing Funnel. They fill out my inquiry form on my website. After some email correspondence, I send them a customized project proposal through my booking system. HoneyBook is my preferred booking system but there are many other options on the market. The client pays a deposit of 1/2 the total amount at the time of booking. The other 1/2 is due one month prior to the wedding date. This balance is completed through a payment portal directly linked between my website and business bank account.

When I show up on the day of the wedding I have already been paid in full. No awkward waiting around for members of the party to scramble to find their wallets. Now, the only money exchange that takes place on the wedding day is the simple matter of a tip, which is often done through a cash app or in a thank you card that is already filled out awaiting my arrival. Before I leave, I give them a small, thoughtful bridal gift. I hop in my car, plug my home address into my favorite GPS app and I'm on my merry way knowing that everything from booking to completion was executed with professional ease.

Before the launch of my website and booking system, I had tangible, printed contracts and I filled in the blanks with a pen. It was a huge step up from the Peasant Stylist and helped to keep me a bit more organized, but clearly I'm not going back to that archaic practice any time soon.

Much improvement, wouldn't you say?

Pricing can be tackled in many different ways. Some stylists and MUAs book a la carte or hourly rates, others by quote, and some by predetermined packages. Let's take a look at each option.

A La Carte:

Benefits to a la carte bookings include giving the bride full freedom to choose which services to book that feel right for her specific needs. By going with an a la carte system, you, as the professional, don't have to structure an entire menu of packages.

I shy away from the à la carte option because I like things to be more streamlined for my bride. If she wants to collect money from each individual bridesmaid that is fine, I am simply removing myself from the equation. There is no need for a middle-man here. I give her one total and a breakdown of how many services will be rendered so there are zero surprises and everything runs smoothly.

I think that this is the most common option used for freelance and bridal beauty business pay structures. If brides are passing some of the glamor service costs on to the bridal party, it's nice to have a breakdown of the exact number of services and total cost per service to show each of them their investment. It literally takes any math or guesswork out of the per-person rate.

Example: Makeup for one bridesmaid = $75 Add lashes = additional $15 Total = $90

Other stylists simplify a bit and charge $90 per face whether they decide to get the lashes or not.

I offer packages instead of pricing out each individual service. I have different packages and add-ons available to customize the pricing according to the bridal parties' needs. This works out great for me and my business. I prefer it to the alacarte method because I've had many bridal parties of yesteryear decide the day of the wedding to not get Emma's hair done and just take care of 6 maids instead of the full roster that was scheduled originally. Then we have the whole situation of "What do I need to refund due to the lesser service count?" blahhhhh.

I like the streamline approach of everything being paid in full before I show up the day of the event and because my packages are a range of people that are taken care of (3 to 5 , 7 to 9 , etc...) there is never any question as to whether I owe money back, because I don't.

Hourly Rates:

Hourly rates seem to keep things simple but I've had clients ask, "what is stopping the stylist from slowing down to make sure she brings in more money?" This is a fair point. Because, of course, the answer is 'nothing'. This isn't a super common option, and I don't find it to be particularly beneficial to me or the client.

Quote:

By quote gives full freedom to you. This option doesn't instill a lot of confidence from your potential client, knowing that you determine a price that isn't explained on your website. Trust is an essential part of the relationship between you and your clients. Again, in their mind, what's stopping you from price gouging or being unfair and up charging as you see fit? You, in turn, could make the argument that they have every right to not book with you if they don't trust your process, but let's avoid that snarkiness if at all possible.

Packages:

I prefer to book packages that make sense for my bridal clientele. I have many options, starting with an elopement package, which was added during the pandemic and the rise of the 'micro-wedding'. I also have medium party size options all the way up to a VIP option that has all the fixins' and covers a very large bridal party and veil placement before the ceremony. I also offer add-ons like travel or an extra person in the bridal party that cover any little gaps in my package options and leave room for special requests as well.

I have a few of my most popular packages posted with pricing on my website. I also send an in-depth pricing brochure via email to prospective brides with additional add-on options and other upgrades they can choose from to customize their experience.

By having a sample of my pricing posted, I give the clients a peek into the price point that I work within. They know before filling out the inquiry form whether I'm in their budget or not. This cuts down on a lot of ghosting and price negotiations later down the road.

How you choose to structure your pricing for your business is obviously completely up to you. If you choose to structure your pricing one way and it doesn't feel right, change it. Not willy-nilly, but please don't feel stuck. Things can always be tweaked as needed. Don't fall victim to the mind set of 'too late, I'm already committed'.

Special Requests:

Some of the special requests I've received over the years have been things like a change of hairstyle between the ceremony and reception, or travel that includes crossing state lines and airfare. I've always handled those types of requests on a situational basis. Usually, if the travel is beyond a couple hours of drive time, I require the bride to pay for the night prior to the wedding at a nearby hotel or the flight cost, etc... Every booking is custom due to the infinitely endless possibilities that could be asked of you.

I always ask for a contact number for the day of the event because of the What-If-Monsters/Apocalypse scenario. What if my car breaks down? I'm certainly not calling the bride to ask her to grab me two miles down the road. I'll be calling the wedding planner or whomever her contact person is. What if the venue's door is locked and the bride is in the shower and unable to get to her phone? I need another option to call so I can be let into the hotel or house or room so I can get set up and started on time no matter what the bride is up to.

If I'm staying for touch ups throughout the reception, I require a seat and a meal. Talk to any veteran photographer, I promise they have a story of why they had to start including this in their contracts. Often their tale will include a cold PBJ in the back hall in between shots because they were treated like third class passengers on the Titanic waiting for their lifeboat during their ten hour booking.

Your services are extremely valuable. Charge your worth.

Remember, the bride's face and hair is in *every* photo. Twenty years post wedding, she will barely remember her centerpieces or the linens or the exact serving set they used to cut the cake. However, she will remember exactly how she looked and felt. It's our job to make sure she looks and feels like the best version of herself. And that, my friends, is worth its weight in gold.

She will have a photo of her wedding day on her mantel and it will probably *not* include her shoes or garter. That mantel piece will showcase the happy couple from the shoulders up, and that is where our magic takes place.

Keep this in mind when considering your pricing.

Charging your worth is a hard nut to crack. I started my own bridal beauty business after being a licensed cosmetologist for many years. I had a few price increases before I made the move to chair rent and entrepreneurship. Those price increases were determined by the commission-based salon I worked at during that time. I'm unsure of how they decided what the new pricing structure was going to look like, all I know is that I had zero to do with the process or the outcome. (More on how and why to set your pricing in the next chapter).

When I was starting to figure out my own pricing structure for Hairpins & Happiness, I was able to reference the old pricing scale from my commission salon, but also wanted a comparative ratio. I started doing a bit of research online and seeing what other stylists included in their pricing structures and what their price points were. I then did a comparative analysis of what I intended to include in my packages and what level of expertise I was able to offer and priced accordingly - according to me, because I answer to no one but me.

There is no right or wrong answer here. However, if you price as a luxury brand and don't deliver a luxury experience you will not succeed at that price point. If you price yourself well below your worth, you will likely either find yourself overlooked OR you'll be overbooked, overworked and eventually burnt out. Also, do not price gouge, that is entirely different than knowing your worth.

What to include in your contract:

You can find a sample contract as a free printout or pdf on my website, but I've put a few bullet points of things that are often overlooked here as well.

Basic Contract Needs:

Couple's names:
Event Date:
Venue address:
How many for hair? How many for makeup?
Call time?
End time?
Total Cost=

Additional Often Overlooked Contract Info:

Photographer & videographer names and social handles?
Photographer's arrival time?
Flower girls?
Do I have permission to post pictures from your event on social media, etc?
Bride's social media handles and tags?
Preferred contact number for the day of the event? Back up number?
Upgrades?

Reflection Questions:

- Do you have a contract in place?

- Is your current contract missing any of the above mentioned overlooked items? What are they?

- Do you identify with the Peasant Stylist from my story?

- What are other bridal stylists charging in your area for similar services?

- What are some of the things in your beauty business that you can upgrade to give your clients a more luxurious experience?

MORE ON PRICING:

Get Out of Your Client's Pockets

Now that we have a grasp on our contracts and pricing let's dive a little deeper, shall we?

Getting out of your client's pockets is an odd concept for a lot of people, so let me explain...

We as hair stylists have no idea what our clients can and can't afford. We don't know their annual salary or what their monthly expenses are. Stop assuming that you know the answers to their financial circumstances.

- Do not tell them what products and services they should buy based on price point.
- Do make suggestions based on what needs they have.
- Do not suggest which products and services are best for their hair based on your preconceived notions of what *they* can or should spend.

Instead, speak to them about what they want done and explain what services are required to achieve the desired outcome. Include pricing, of course, but only as part of the conversation, not as an end-all /be-all.

When a client asks me what I used on their hair to 'make it so smooth,' I tell them. I don't tell them and then immediately say "... but it's really expensive! You should get this one, it's a lot cheaper."

What a slap in their face. If someone said that to me I would assume one of three things.

1- The stylist couldn't afford the product themselves.
2- The stylist assumes that I am a charity case and I'm so broke that I can't afford the *good* stuff.
3- If it's SO expensive and the cheaper option is fine, why does the hairstylist carry the pricey option at all?

No matter which they assume, it's not a good look. Frankly, it's quite condescending.

On the other hand, if they ask if there is something else comparable but less expensive, then you can give the less expensive option and explain the differences and your preferences as a stylist.

The same principle applies to pricing out salon services and bridal parties. Stop undercutting your pricing because you *feel* bad for charging your worth.

Emotional Discounting can be a tough habit to break.

We fear that the client will say no. We fear that they can't spend that amount we quote. We fear that they won't book with us. We often feel bad for charging what we're worth, so we give discounts and freebies to help cope with that fear.

Do not give Emotional Discounts.

Instead, give the client the base price and offer upgrades, or give the total amount and offer lesser services for a smaller price point. Offer the lesser service/ smaller price tag option *only* if the potential client inquires about it first.

Example:
Betty inquires about you taking care of her and her bridal party's hair on the day of her wedding. She has a total of 6 women needing hair styling and 1 flower girl. Your total cost, including

a hair trial/preview and your travel fee, is $800.

Her reaction to that price is something along the lines of, "Oh, wow. I didn't expect it to cost that much. Can you do it for $600 instead?"

What is your knee-jerk reaction? Are your palms sweating just thinking about this awkward interaction?

I've been there.

Once upon a time, this Peasant Stylist used to bend and meet them in the middle. I have been caught in the realm of 'I really loved her whole vision and really wanted to work with her photographer again'. This circumstance can be difficult.

I'm not trying to shame you. We as professionals need to stand up for ourselves, though.

Let's ask ourselves: Would this same client try to get a lesser price for her dental work if her dentist quoted the same $800? Probably not. That's actually a laughable suggestion, isn't it? The truth is, it's not the $800 dollar price tag that's the problem. The problem is that she isn't finding *value* in your work and/or time.

Instead of automatically jumping to sweaty palms and apologizing, let's instead give scalable options that help maintain your professionalism.

"Where there is no struggle, there is no strength."
-Oprah Winfrey

You get to decide what those options are. Perhaps they pay X now and settle up for X later. You could also suggest taking away the flower girl and bridal preview to tweak the price back to $650. You could offer for the party to come to your salon instead of you going on location.

Giving a discount without any reduction on their end discredits your professional integrity and short changes your business in the process.

I'm at a point in my career that I will stand my ground and stick to my original pricing that was quoted. Quite frankly, if this client doesn't book with me then there'll be another one that will. That future bride will not only book me, but she'll also be elated to pay my prices because she can see the value in my time and expertise.

Do what's best for you. Think creatively without being a doormat and letting the potential client walk all over you. As my coworker Ali recently stated so eloquently, "We have to find the sweet spot between being a dick and a doormat."

Keep these four things in mind when setting your pricing...

- Materials -
Figure out the cost of materials and the amount needed to provide said services.

If you were a florist you would need to price out the cost for the centerpieces and bouquets, right? How much does each bloom, vase, wire, twine, ribbon, and floral tape cost going into your proposal?

It's no different for a bridal hair stylist. Think about your bobby pins, elastics, hairspray, and other products that go into creating an up style. The more luxurious the brands, the higher the pricing has to be to cover the cost of those products and materials.

- Expenses-
How much money do you spend monthly on things like business cards, internet, electricity, and gas to get you from location to location? Also, think about how many bookings it takes to cover

all of these expenditures.

- Time Investment-

Your time is worth something too! We love our careers but should still be compensated for the valuable services we provide. Hours, not only on the day of booking but also learning and perfecting our craft, replying to emails and drawing up contracts should be accounted for here.

- Demand-

If you're booked out really far in advance this means you're in high demand and need to price accordingly. If your calendar is filling up 9, 12 and 18+ months out then demand is high.

Repeat after me, "I am a professional and my artistic work is valuable."

Story Time:

Have you ever heard the popular urban legend about Picasso and his million-dollar napkin?

Pablo Picasso was once confronted by an admirer of his work while in a Paris market. She asked him if he could do a quick sketch for her on a café napkin. Picasso nodded his head politely in agreement and went to work on the napkin. When he handed the napkin back to the woman, he also asked her for one million Francs in exchange for the sketch.

The woman was of course appalled at the request; "How can you ask for so much money when it only took you five minutes to draw this?"

"No," Picasso replied, "It took me 40 years to draw this in five minutes."

What can we take away from this story? Experience matters. While your clients and brides may only *see* you work for a few hours and it *seems* as though you haven't spent a lot of time on their hair, the truth is that it took years of practice, thousands of mistakes and hours of work to master your craft.

Picasso knew his value. He generously gave his time and talent to create something beautiful. People seem to forget the endless hours of practice it takes to perfect what we do and make it seem effortless. We, as creatives, need to charge accordingly. Maybe not Picasso amounts of money, but hey, on the other hand, maybe!?

Upsell your services

I offer upgrades to all my brides. Think about it. If you eat dinner at a high end, candlelit restaurant, any server will ask at the end of the meal, "Did we save some room for dessert?" They ask every single time, at every restaurant. That's not a coincidence. That, my friends, is the fancy version of, "wanna add fries to that?" Every successful business offers upgrades. Why should we be any different?

What kind of upgrades you ask? You could have a VIP package that includes touch ups throughout the evening or veil placement at the ceremony venue. You can include the bridal preview as a larger 'all inclusive' package or complimentary bridal gift with your 'Golden Hour' package. Be creative, the sky's the limit! It doesn't have to feel pushy or 'salesy'. If the upsell you're offering is enticing to the bride, she'll gladly upgrade with little to no hesitation...

Upselling is the natural next step and an easy way to add value to your services and more money in your pocket. Don't sell yourself short by overlooking this step.

> ## "Luxury brands aren't cheap and cheap brands aren't luxurious."
> ### -Unknown

Note: You need to find your sweet spot. Take into consideration what your local competition is charging for similar services. I'm not saying you should copy and paste their pricing brochure. What I am saying is that you don't want to set your prices so high that you price yourself out of business, or be so low and inexpensive that potential brides assume you're inexperienced and desperate for work.

The answers to the following questions are your sweet spot for pricing:

- If every hair stylist on earth charged the same exact price, what would make a bride inclined to choose me?

- What makes me unique?

- What makes me more desirable than the competition?

- How much does it cost for me to provide a single updo or makeup application?

- What can I do to increase my demand?

- What are my total monthly expenses for my business?

- How much time do I have invested in a bridal party *before* I show up on the day of the event?

- What sets me apart from my competitors?

- What makes my business special enough to stand out from the crowd?

YOUR BRIDAL KIT:

A Checklist.

Now that you have the bridal booking, what do you need to take with you?

Any booking, whether it be a wedding, photo shoot, or fashion show can be extremely hectic and full of surprises. A well-curated bridal kit can help you smoothly navigate any debacle, big or small. I'm sure that you already have curling irons and hairspray, but what else do you need in your hair kit to ensure that you're well prepared for the day's booking and whatever it has to throw at you?

Let's start with the obvious...

Tools:

- flat iron
- 1" curling iron
- 2" curling iron
- blow dryer
- shears
- rat tail comb
- teasing brush and/or comb
- detangling comb
- detangling brush and/or Wet brush
- round brushes in multiple sizes
- 4 or more jaw clips
- double prong detail clips

- hand mirror

Products:

- strong hold hairspray
- light hold workable finishing spray
- dry shampoo
- texture powder
- humidity protectant
- dry wax spray
- molding paste
- volumizing mousse
- smoothing serum
- pomade

Now for the not so obvious...

- extension cord
- back up flat iron
- cash
- a few dazzly bits
- safety pins
- phone charger
- pen and paper
- lint roller
- small scissors
- hand sanitizer
- Mr. Rogers sweater
- topsy tail
- safety pins
- lash glue and nail glue
- personal items ie: feminine products, etc...
- large craft needle and 'hair colored' thread
- back up cans of favorite strong hold and workable finishing sprays

Consumables : you will forever be buying and replacing your stock...

- ample amount of regular size bobby pins
- large bobby pins
- hairpins
- small elastics
- large hair ties
- hair donuts or padding
- business cards
- mints
- snacks

Optional items include but are not limited to...

- collapsible chair
- portable table
- ring light and stand
- kitchen sink
- a kazoo

Let me dive into a couple of things and explain myself a bit further...

$$$:

Bringing some cash for yourself is also part of the 'be prepared for anything' mantra.

This career takes you on location to all corners of Timbuktu and back. Once I was on location up in some remote area of Michigan's Upper Peninsula and needed gas. They didn't take credit. I shit you not, I didn't believe it either at first. To my relief, I had my handy cash stash!

Things happen. Be prepared for the bizarre.

A Beautiful Day in the Neighborhood:

The Mr. Roger's sweater is a necessity. I have had back to back bookings where the first venue is frigid as a meat locker in January and the second is sickeningly stuffy and hotter than Hades. Simply, you just never know if you'll be too warm or cold.

A true professional would never skip a beat over something so easily avoidable. Being a Midwest girl I am used to having to dress in layers due to the inevitable crazy weather fluctuations. Dressing in a lightweight shirt and layering with a jacket or sweater that you can still work comfortably in, is the sensible thing to do. And yes, the Mr. Rogers' reference is yet another reminder of my Xennial roots. Deal.

Topsy-What?:

If you haven't already Googled what a Topsy Tail is, it's a plastic comb-sized tool with a large loop in it, resembling an oversized, floppy sewing needle. Traditionally, in the 1990's it was used to twist a ponytail inside out by pulling it through the center. I often use it to fish misplaced pieces of hair through another so as not to disrupt the finished up style. It's handy for finishing work and detail pieces.

Personal Items:

Ladies know that it's always nice to pay it forward, especially, in the case of someone needing a feminine product. Having them on hand in your bridal kit (as well as safety pins, nail glue, and other items that fix oopsies) is just a small part of always being prepared for the 'what if's' in life. These items aren't heavy or cumbersome and are easily stored in a small pocket in your kit. I highly recommend having these things on hand - you may just save someone's day!

Hot Tip for Hair Donuts:

Hair donuts straight out of the package are large and dense. When using them on someone with short or fine hair texture they can be difficult to hide, due to their obvious shape and size. Instead, take the few anchor stitches out of the donut and unroll it. Now cut the long tube of synthetic wefting into 2" to 4" sections. You can use as few or as many of these smaller donuts as you want on the inside of an upstyle, to bulk up the hair-mass.

This is easier to use and more customizable for each client's hair texture, wants, and needs.

The Great Chair Debate:

I do not travel with a chair but I know many stylists that do. If you tend to do more makeup than hair, this may be more relevant for you so that you don't have to stoop down while applying a face. Let's save our necks and backs when we can, people!

If you primarily do hair, you really don't need to fuss with it unless you're a shorty or walk on stilts. Most venues have a chair option that works. Worse-case scenario, I've had to have clients sit sideways on a high backed chair so that I can reach their napes. For as infrequently as it's been an issue over my career, I am willing to take the gamble that there will be adequate seating options available. I feel that dealing with the unknown outweighs the strife of dealing with lugging an awkward chair all over God's green earth.

What it all comes down to is your willingness to go with the flow and adapt, or come prepared for the unlikely. The choice is ultimately yours.

The Case Itself:

I have had many different vessels to lug my bridal kit in over the years. I had a duffle bag with wheels at one point that sounded good in theory, but I didn't end up loving it. I have had multiple shoulder bags and carrying cases in a wide variety of styles. I have recently found a new shoulder bag with a structured hard bottom. I'm loving it for all of my sprays and products because they can stand up and not run the risk of spilling over while in transit. I also found a beautiful case with lots of zippers and compartments to keep my tools and consumables neat and tidy! The link to my new fave can be found in my stories on both fb and instagram, and on my website at

HairpinsAndHappiness.com.

Never Run Out:

I still have a bit of PTSD after the great bobby pin shortage of 2020. Ummm... yesss, this was a real thing. Covid created a lot of supply chain issues and the beauty industry was no exception.

There were none. No bobby pins. Backordered everywhere.

I was on a hunt for weeks to get even just a sleeve of 25 from Goody at the SuperMart. Target? Sold out. Ulta? Sold out. Sally's Beauty Supply? Laughed at me. Every professional beauty vendor was backordered until forever in the Midwest. I was panic stricken y'all! This is a necessary tool of my trade.

I had this apocalyptic scenario in my head of offering my upcoming brides a 'bridal scrunchie' in lieu of their practiced upstyles of choice.

I know you're thinking "But all the weddings were canceled during the pandemic."

Many were canceled. Several rescheduled. Some decided to move forward safely and still wanted to get prettied up for their intimate backyard/Skype/live feed/Facetime weddings. We wore masks, washed our hands often, and still needed bobby pins.

I had always been well stocked in the past. Post Covid, I am beyond well stocked and have probably entered the realm of obsessiveness about my bobby pins. I have hoards of one pound boxes of pins in a closet, just in case. I will never disclose their location. I don't have a problem, *you* have a problem.

Let this be a lesson.

"On a long journey, even a straw weighs heavy."
- Spanish Proverb

I hope this list has helped you to prep your bridal kit. Remember, you have to lug everything you pack back and forth. If you don't need the bulky ring light stand, don't bring it. You can probably skip that kitchen sink as well. Too bulky. Kazoo? Read the room.

The point is to be streamlined, professional, and well-prepared.

Happy packing!!

Questions:

- Is there anything in this chapter that you hadn't thought of adding to your kit? Is it now waiting in your Amazon cart?

- Do you plan to take your own chair with you on location? Dear Gawd, why?

- How many boxes of bobby pins is too many? If you think you have too many, add more. Come to the support group, Tuesdays and Thursdays.

BRIDZILLAS:

Almost Always a Bridesmaid

Bridezilla:
Noun; Informal
A soon-to-be bride who is overly involved with the details of the wedding and becomes extremely self-centered, demanding or otherwise difficult to tolerate.
- Dictionary.com

A Zilla can take on many shapes. It is a rarity that I have dealt with a true "Bridezilla". I'm not saying never, I'm just saying that typically it's not the bride. If there is, it's pretty much always a bridesmaid.

I'm often asked about 'Bridezillas'.

"How can you deal with all the Bridezillas!?"

"I bet you have some crazy Bridezilla stories, huh?"

Truth is they are far and few between. In my twenty years of serving brides and their bridal parties, I have come across literally 2 brides that I would deem Bridezillas.

Don't get me wrong, those two were whoppers! But, overall, it's very rarely a bride that turns out to be crazy on a wedding day. It's always a Maid-Zilla, Mom-Zilla or even an Aunt-Zilla!

We have all been made aware of this erratic 'Zilla' behavior through television shows like 'Bridezillas' and 'Say Yes To The

Dress'. Always a drama queen in every episode.

My definition of a 'Zilla' : Someone that thrives on attention and can't stand when they're not in the spotlight. Someone that acts irrationally and emotionally to every detail of the event or situation.

I truly do not believe it's an intentional act. As a rule, I believe that these 'Zillas' are acting out of stress and concern. Mostly stress that they've made up in their own minds. By the day of the wedding all the details are set. What will be will be. As rational adults, we know this. Systems are in place and what was overlooked will have to be just that, an oversight. (So long as it isn't on our part as the beauty professionals!!)

The little 'what-if monsters' that lurk in the deepest corners of every woman's mind...

What if I forget my speech?

What if the car breaks down?

What if something spills on my dress?

What if the other bridesmaids look prettier than me?

What if the other mom looks better than me?

What if we all choose the *same* hairstyle?

What if we all want *different* hair styles?

What if the bar doesn't stock my favorite vodka?

What if we run out of time?

What if I don't like my makeup?

What if a plane goes overhead during the wedding and no one can hear the officiant?

What if the dress that I had altered and fit specifically to my body last week doesn't fit anymore like in the crazy nightmare I had and I have to walk down the aisle naked?

What if my nose falls off my face?

Take a deep breath.

These 'what-if monsters' are typical of anyone that has planned a large event. Thankfully, not everyone acts on them or obsesses over them. As a matter of fact, most people don't. The one Zilla that does act on them is a pest. This we can be certain. We, as the professionals in the room, can't let it ruin the day for everyone else.

Normally, the bride is fully aware of the usual suspect that would turn into a Zilla. I've been told time and time again to 'watch for Aunt Millie' or 'don't listen to Nancy'.

About a decade ago the bridal party coined a phrase to act as a warning in case their resident Zilla was being a nuisance. The phrase of choice came from the packaging of the hair extensions we were incorporating into the bride's hair style. The package read 'Color: Jamaican Spice'.

Any time our Zilla was riding the crazy train, one of us would start talking about the extension's color and someone else would catch on and give the Zilla a chore; something to distract or remove her from the bride's immediate space.

This was so effective that I've outwardly suggested choosing a safe phrase or codeword to other brides when they were warning me of their party's potential Zilla.

The code word really helped with the good cop/ bad cop policing of the situation. If I need to be the bad cop to help redirect a Zilla, I will.

You are more than welcome to borrow 'Jamaican Spice' or help your bridal party come up with one that is unique to them and their day. I've also heard code words like 'Pineapple' and 'Shoop'.

The codeword is meant to be a fun tool to ease the anxiety in the room. Have fun with it!!

More often than not this isn't necessary. Mostly, my bridal parties are filled with funny and smart family members and friends that are enthusiastic about helping the happy couple celebrate their marriage!

On a very rare occasion, the Zilla you encounter on a wedding day may not be a member of the bridal party or their family at all. I had the *pleasure* of working with a condescending hell-witch of a MUA once.

We both showed up for our booking simultaneously. The venue was an absolutely gorgeous beach house. The MOB directed me toward a floor to ceiling corner window overlooking the lake. It had an enormous marble table, natural light, chairs, and outlets - all the things a beauty pro could hope for.

I waited for the MUA to lug her kit inside before setting up for myself, because that's the polite thing to do. When I asked the MUA if she would prefer that I set up to the right, preserving the most natural light for her from the ginormous window to the left, she looked annoyed.

She contorted her face with disgust and said, "Actually.... if you could just set up, like.... over there somewhere that'd be great. I get migraines from the hairspray." She fully extended her arm and with a flip of the wrist, a wave of her fingers, and a hiss of her tongue, gestured toward a small folding table in the shadowy corner of the room.

Ya'll, she actually waved me away like I was an obnoxious mosquito! Whhaaat? Did she really think that scooching me to a corner six feet away was going to keep the smell of hair products away from her?

* * *

Public Service Announcement:

If you're that sensitive to the smell of any beauty product,
you may be in the wrong profession. You will not
avoid all beauty products at any booking. There is zero
promise that there will be separate rooms for multiple
beauty pros to work in, adequate ventilation, or enough
space to spread out. It's the nature of the beast.

I must've looked like I had just been slapped across the face. I really didn't know how to respond other than to kill the hell-witch with kindness.

"Yep, I'm fine so long as I have an outlet and a chair!" I smiled, making eye contact with half the bridal party that was equally shocked at the makeup artist's snobbish behavior as I made my way across the room.

I made the most of my third class ticket seating and went to work setting up my shadowy hair station. I can only assume that the MUA must've realized how patronizing she had sounded and in an attempt to redeem herself added, "Do you need any help moving the table? You *could* come a little closer to the window."

"Nope. I'm great right here! I can be very flexible!" I said and smiled back at her. (My inner dialogue was saying, "Oh, you'll *permit* me to come closer, your majesty!? You're too kind.")

"Well, you know, you should really do what's best for you and your business," she said in her uppity tone.

I just kept plugging away at my task at hand, seemingly unphased by her venomous remarks.

Piano. Piano.

Now I don't know if you believe in Karma but if this isn't immediate Karma, I don't know what is. While starting my second head of hair of the morning I noticed the MUA frantically looking around and then grabbing her keys and bolting out the door. I assumed she ran out to her car but when she didn't come back for a while the bridesmaids started talking amongst themselves.

She had forgotten her mascara. She had <u>none</u> in her kit. I shit you not. Instant Karma.

Being the ray of sunshine that I am, my response to the situation was, "Oh, no! I wish I would've known before she left for SuperMart. I have my makeup kit in my car, it's stocked with at least 3 or 4 waterproof mascaras. She certainly could have borrowed some of mine!"

I did mean what I said, I definitely would've let her borrow. Not to help her but to help the bridal party. I felt a wave of redemption when I was able to hypothetically save the day.

When she returned to the venue she was visibly frazzled and kept reminding everyone in the room of how quickly she ran out and bought SuperMart mascara to save her own arse. It was pitifully comical, really.

This experience reminded me of how lucky I am to get to work with so many talented and kind vendors on a regular basis! For this I am endlessly grateful!

The Zilla Wedding Vendor happens extremely infrequently. I can truly only think of this specific instance that it has *ever* happened, actually. (Someone should go back and read chapter #2 on professionalism, no?) As a rule, our industry is full of professionals wanting to help promote one another. It behooves us to help and uplift other wedding vendors. It makes us look UNprofessional to be catty and condescending. We are not in competition with one another. We have been hired to glam up the loved ones of the happy couple. Spread happiness <u>not</u> cattiness.

"Throw some perm on your attitude.
Girl, you gotta relax!"
-Bruno Mars, Perm

Most brides, vendors, and bridal parties are a delight to work with. On the off chance that you do have to deal with a Zilla here are a few helpful tips...

1- Keep your cool.

Do not get snarky or short tempered no matter the situation. It isn't worth coming down to their level of childish behavior. Don't let it show outwardly that their poor behavior is getting to you. I will often take on the actions of a toddler's mom, trying to slowly and calmly talk them off the ledge, "Yes, we can do those fun things if you eat your vegetables first..."

2- Smile!

A little honey goes a long way!

3- Guide

Help to steer the Zilla into another direction or divert their negative behavior.
What I mean is this: If a Zilla is nit-picking something about their hair or the bride's hair, or whatever the situation, calmly but firmly take control back. Inform them of the options to tweak their style and move forward. Piano, Piano.

Obviously, I do not expect that if you're dealing with a true Zilla that you'll always be able to take control of the situation. Don't add to the drama by gossiping about the Zilla.
In my experience the bridal party mostly helps dissolve the chaos before it takes over the entire mood of the day. Just know that you are more than capable of helping to navigate a Zilla moment.

Let's all cross our fingers that we won't have to navigate a Zilla situation anytime in the near future. But also know that if you do have a Zilla state of affairs, you can and will help diffuse the Zilla bomb!

Things to Ponder:

- Have you ever dealt with a Zilla? Would you do anything differently?

- What are some of the 'what-if monsters' that haunt you as a professional hairstylist?

- What is your go to safe word?

PERSONALITY TYPES:

Bride Tribe

Now that we've gotten through some of the more mundane aspects of our chosen profession, let us have some fun!

Let's talk about all the various characters that can come to play while we as the beauty professionals are glamming up the bridal party.

We as humans know that there are many distinctive types of people in this world. Different personalities that we can appreciate for different reasons. We all have friend groups that don't necessarily get along with the other important people in our lives. Personalities clash for whatever reason and they just don't click. That's okay.

When a group of individuals are all forced together to celebrate one special person in their lives, things can get hairy. Coworkers, childhood friends, college friends, family members and soon to be family members all squishing into one space for the duration of the wedding morning can be interesting, to say the least! There are always a handful of these characters involved in the getting ready process. Some are good and others not so good, but no matter what the circumstance, no matter how schmancy the shindig, they come to play!

Their real names have been changed to protect the Innocent. It's me. I'm the Innocent.

Henceforth, they shall be known as: Picky Polly, Beauty Guru

Becky, Laid Back Lana, No Drama Mama, Quickie Queen, Hype Girl Hailey, Potato Pam, Rally Girl Rhonda, and Biggest Fan.

I'm going to start with the most difficult, and work my way up into the lovies.

Picky Polly

Polly knows what she wants. Or, *thinks* she knows what she wants. Strike that. Actually, Polly is picky to the point of knowing, changing, tweaking, fixing, and still unsure if it looks exactly like the picture that she "knows" that she wants.

I once had a Polly as one of the bridesmaids in a large party that really sticks out to me, even years later. This particular Polly had come into the salon weeks before her brother's wedding to have a trial run of her own hair and makeup. (That's not a thing. Normally the bride and occasionally the MOB are the only ones to have a preview.)

… it went a little something like this…

Polly and the bride both came into the salon to do a bridal preview. One clearly didn't understand that it wasn't her day, but I digress. Can you guess who? Polly insisted that she go first because the bride was probably nervous about going first. This did not seem to be the case, but this was our first encounter, so what did I know? She threw a few inspiration photos at me quickly, explaining that she has terrible hair and awful skin, and that she has never once liked anything that any stylist in her entire life has ever done.

Great. I was literally set up for failure.

She brought *all* of her own makeup because she didn't trust that I would have the correct shade of *anything* for her "oh, so very special" skin tone. She was very much a fair caucasian person with zero oddities to her complexion, but again, what did I know?

The hair portion of the program went smoothly. I pinned her waist-grazing blonde locks up into a low chignon that she seemed to be pleased with. She gave rave reviews like, "This is fine, I guess," and "I'll have to see if it actually stays in. My hair always falls out."

Piano, piano.

Next came the makeup application. She displayed all of her very high-end Chanel and MAC products across my salon station. She proceeded to meticulously explain to me what to do with each product, "You put this here using this brush and sweep it up this direction and then you use this but just a dab or it's way too much and you'll have to completely start over..." It felt very much like I was getting reprimanded for something I hadn't even done yet.

Super fun, let me tell ya!

When it came to her bronzer, she lost her ever-loving mind. This 'bronzer' was actually a highlighter. It had zero warmth to it, whatsoever. It was more of a silver or pewter than a bronze, if you can picture that. I swept the shimmery shade across her cheekbones and bridge of her nose as she instructed. She immediately lifted the hand mirror and scoffed, "That's *obviously* not enough. I need to look *tan!*"

I dipped the soft bristled blush brush back into the pallet and reapplied for a second time.

"Still not enough," she sneered with a disgusted roll of the eye.

I did a third and forth application of *her* product the way *she* was instructing me to and it still was not enough, because the shade obviously offered zero warmth or tanning effect due to its silvery tone.

She grabbed the pallet and brush, vigorously swirled the bristles into the 'bronzer' and shoved it back into my hand.

"Here. This might *actually* work now. You didn't have enough on the brush."

Note: Clearly everyone hearing this story is thinking 'I can't imagine allowing this girl to treat me like this.' Retrospect, I 100% agree. In the moment, I was on autopilot, just trying to get through it so that I could move on to the sweet bride's services. But, as all things in life, we live and we learn! And let me just say, never again will I allow for such blatant disrespect.

After the fifth and final application of the same damn product being layer-caked onto her face, she lifted the hand mirror to reinspect 'my' work and immediately recoiled at the sight of herself.

"Oh. My. Gawd! What did you do?? I look like an oompa-loompa! I'm completely orange now!"

My knee-jerk response was, "There. Is. No. Warmth. In. This. Product. Crazy-train!"

I didn't really say that. But wasn't that satisfying for a hot second? I actually responded with stunned silence. She marched off to the bathroom, where she removed her makeup and reapplied it to her satisfaction.

I moved on to take care of my lovely, level headed bride. She assured me that I had done nothing wrong, and that her soon to be sister-in-law tends to always air on the side of the dramatic.

Good luck with that!

Cut to the day of the wedding:

I was mad at myself for the amount of anxiety this particular Polly had caused. I am well aware of my capabilities and rarely feel any stress leading up to a booking. She had me overthinking every silly little detail of the preview and I was dreading having to go through any of that again.

I arrived at the hotel and I set up in a spacious banquet room that the MOB and FOB had reserved for the morning's festivities. They had a lovely continental breakfast spread out to one side of the large boardroom table and I had the other end to set up for glamming up the gals.

Polly made the decision to take care of her own makeup but still demanded that she go first for hair because, "My hair always takes the most time."

She sat down in the cushioned hotel chair and looked around frantically. "Where's the mirror." She said this *at* me while looking over her shoulder.

I calmly explained that all I had was a hand mirror.

"How are you supposed to do my hair without a mirror for me to see?" she sneered.

"You don't need to see. I do." An abrupt answer, but I was over her shenanigans.

"I just had two inches taken off my length sooo, I don't really know if you'll be able to get it up into an updo or not. You know what I mean?"

Her hair length was closer to her elbow than her bicep even with the two inches gone. "I think we'll be just fine."

I put her hair up into a similar low chignon as the one we had practiced, with a few minor adjustments upon her request. She huffed and continuously checked in the hand mirror, but allowed me to do my job.

After she was taken care of and I had been *allowed* to move onto the other lovies in the group, she kept asking anyone with ears if it looked okay.

"Are you sure?" "What do you think?" "Is my hair alright?" "But don't you think I should wear it down, instead?" "I don't know.

Don't you think I should have her redo this part?"

As heart warming as it was to listen to her discredit my work over and over, It was then that I realized she wasn't picky so much as she was actually uncertain of *herself.*

Most of the time when people are this picky to the point of self doubt, they have little to no self confidence. These people need compliments and they thrive on attention.They need affirmation. She wasn't trying to be bitchy. She was trying to be accepted, like a little girl on the elementary school playground trying to fit in. She just wants to be told she looks pretty. She was clearly going about it in the wrong way, but still.

Polly kept disappearing for blocks of time and then reappearing and asking the same people all the same questions about her hair. The entire bridal party kept reassuring me that it wasn't anything I had done. I just replied with a gentle smile and answered, "I know."

Polly approached the bride while I was doing her hair.

"Umm, can I talk to you for a second? It's about my hair," she said in a staged whisper, while simultaneously pointing at me, in what she must have thought was an inconspicuous manner. (If she had any designs on being a spy in the future, she would be busted immediately. Remember: I'm physically touching the bride's hair. If she can hear Polly, so can I).

The bride snipped back for the first time throughout all of this madness, "Just say what you need to say. I'm getting my hair done for *my* wedding right now. It's *my* turn."

With high eyebrows and a timid and childish tone she said, "Well, ummm... I just wanted to know if you'd mind if I went up to my room and showered? I think I'm just going to wear my hair down and straight for the day. Do you care? Orrrrr....?"

"Not really. You do what you need to do. The rest of us all have our hair done up but if you really need to shower then you do that."

The bride kept her gaze straight forward, never once looking in Polly's direction. She was so over her antics by this point.

"Okay, I will." Polly replied, and off she went up to her hotel room to undo the updo.

Everyone else in the party was horrified at Polly's self absorbed behavior and kept reassuring me that they all felt beautiful and loved my work.

When the getting-ready portion of the morning was starting to wrap up, I asked all the girls if they needed anything. This is when we shellac everyone one last time and tweak any pins that may seem troublesome, etc. During this time Polly had the audacity to come up to me and ask, "Can you just flat iron the back again for me? I don't want to look frizzy."

To which I replied, "I think it looks fine." and I hit her with a quick mist of hairspray and ran my hand down the back of her hair with a quick swipe. Quite frankly, she's lucky I didn't *literally* hit her with the hairspray can.

During this era of my career I didn't know the importance of having a full contract in place, nor did I require prepayment before the day of the wedding. This is one of many scenarios that helped to teach me why these things are so important.

Polly was refusing payment. "I didn't even like it," she said. Since she wasn't wearing the style I gave her, she wasn't going to pay for it. After that she never once stepped foot back in the glamour room. She was hiding.

The bridal party all pitched in to help pay for Polly's hair because she was refusing to. Their kindness was a lovely reminder that there are good people in this world.

Although this is a very dramatic version of a Picky Polly, they are often one of the bridal party attendees. Just be grateful when Polly doesn't show up!

Beauty Guru Becky

Often confused with Picky Polly is our Beauty Guru Becky. Becky can have a picky tendency, but in addition, she is more likely going to educate you throughout the morning. She knows all the current trends, and questions whether you are following the latest influencers and beauty brands.

Becky informs you, who is the actual professional, how to approach doing her hair.

She'll say things like, "Do you have a wand? A curling wand is really the only way to get *my* hair to hold, but of course you knew that, I'm sure," with a distrusting, toothy smile.

Becky is also a habitual 'fixer'. Always running her hands through her hair and tugging at the bangs that she reminded you to put extra volume in because, "they always fall no matter what the hairstylist does."

Imagine that. Your hair doesn't stay curled the way it was styled when you are constantly raking your hands through it, pulling on it, messing with your fringe, tucking it behind your ear after you've told me over and over that you *never* tuck your hair, blah, blah, blah...

... Shocking!! (Insert aggressive eye roll. One day my eyes are going to stick that way)

That's where the similarities to Polly end. Becky is more dangerous, because she will insert herself into my other clients' consultations the morning of the wedding. She is usually looked to as the beauty/fashion aficionado of the group, even if that's only in her own mind.

She offers helpful advice like, "You always hate when you wear your hair up, leave it down this time," and "I think you look better with it more off your face," or "She always needs a bit more lift at the crown."

My favorite is when a bridesmaid is elated with how they look and Becky chimes in with a confident, "Well, she looks okay but I think the side could be a little smoother, don't you? I mean I know you're the professional but it looks a little messy or something doesn't it?"

So, now Becky is having me redo the other bridesmaid's hair too? Whaaaat!?

Navigating the Beckys and Pollys of a bridal party can be overwhelming, especially as a rookie stylist. Please remember to hold your ground, and be polite but not a pushover. If you're exuding confidence in what you do and start offering just as much feedback and helpful advice as Becky, you'll win the room over and gain their trust. Also, bear in mind that although these two players come to the party often, it's not *always*.

You can simultaneously be prepared for the worst and anticipate the best case scenario.

As a stark contrast to those two characters there are always the lovies!

For instance, **Laid Back Lana** is the most amazing bridesmaid to work with! You can spot her easily because she'll be the one that arrives on time and ready to jump in and help. Not in a pushy or know-it-all, frantic way, but in a genuinely helpful mother-earth kinda way.

When Lana sits in your chair she often says things like, "I trust you. Do whatever you think!"
and she truly means it. Even so, make sure to talk to Lana about basics like if she wants any hair down to frame her face and what her jewelry and dress's neckline look like. After a minimal amount of information collecting, do your thing! Be creative!

This is the dream client that lets you stretch your creativity and then is floored at your unparalleled talent and showers you with genuine compliments after the fact. You'll want to fold her up and put her in your pocket to save for later in life if you ever need a lift! She's the best confidence booster evvvvvver! Embrace it! We will always love a Laid Back Lana!!

Another lovie that often accompanies a bride tribe is a **No Drama Momma**.

This character has a couple of littles who are either in the wedding as a ring bearer or flower girl, or simply hanging in the room with Momma. She participates in the festivities, but never makes the morning about her little people. She effortlessly handles what needs to be done,
stepping away occasionally to do things like feeding her child or helping another family member (MOB, Groomsmen, friend of the family, etc...), while remembering that the day is about the couple's wedding.

When it's her turn to sit in my chair she'll often mimic Lana and say things like, "As long as it's all up and out of my way, you can do whatever you want!" And again, she means it.

Our **Quickie Queens** tend to be on the high-strung end of the spectrum. These Queens tend to race about trying to help, and tend to do things they haven't always been asked to do, like an unpaid coordinator. They are overwhelmed by the day's events and can't find the calm. What these Queens really need is a slow deep breath, an old-fashioned 'nerve tonic,' or an actual quickie, but they typically don't recognize this in themselves. Our Quickie Queens are like Bobble Heads constantly wiggling and turning to talk to someone or check the time.

Queenie will sit in your chair with visible sweat on their brow from racing around doing little tasks and chores that they've taken upon themselves. Queenie says things like, "Okay, we have to make this pretty fast because I don't know who is going to go locate the groom's shoes!"

Side note - those shoes aren't even misplaced. They're under his jacket in the corner. Even if they were missing, people can still get married without them. Nobody is marrying the shoes, they're marrying the person in them. There is plenty of time in the morning's timeline to take care of everyone on the list, including this Queen. She has created this sense of urgency because she is Fidgets McJivets and can't sit still.

Simply do your job and do it well.

Speak to her like you're trying to coax a high-strung kitten down from a tree: with stark raving level-headedness. It's part of your job to maintain a fun atmosphere in the room, so try to convince her in the short time you have with her that all will be well. If you can't, just know that you tried your best and that at a minimum, her hair and/or makeup looked amazing!

Hype Girl Hailey is another fun archetype, but for completely different reasons than the sensible Lanas and Mommas. Hailey is a positive force and also has a party girl vibe that everyone gravitates toward!

Hailey greets everyone with a smile and a warm hug. She has all the fun goofy stories and quips to lighten the mood throughout the getting ready process. She is always ready to pour the mimosas! She pitches in when she can, and doesn't think of tasks as a chore, but instead as a part of her lovely friend's day! She is a social butterfly so she may be difficult to nail down to your chair, but once you do, you have an upbeat conversation and she's fun to work with.

As soon as her glam services are complete, Hailey will jump up and compliment your work, telling everyone how amazing the glam team is and that she's never felt better about her reflection!

"Oh, My, Gawd! I look ammmmaaaazzzing!! How did you guys do this? It's exactly what I wanted! You guys are SO talented, I can't stop staring at myself!" She will continue the love fest with every other service completed, yelling across the room to make sure every single bridesmaid gets her just compliments. Major ego booster!

PS: This is the gal you want to swap socials with because she will be the one to sing your praises to all her peeps on the interwebs as well as in person!

Unfortunately, as a rule, there isn't more than one Hailey on hand at a time. The universe decided that too many Hailey's in a room would make the world implode. So make the most of these ladies because they're the gals that you and other stylists will chat about later! "Remember the girl that was walking around the room giving everyone a sample of the vodka whip cream? Straight from the can to their mouths!? She was hilarious!! I'd love to hang out with her again!!"

To round things out nicely we have to talk about **Potato Pam**. She unfortunately tends to look and act much like, you guessed it, a potato. I'm not saying this to be mean. She is who she is. Not everyone can be a charming sweet Lana, Hailey or Momma... some people have to just be a potato. Just be thankful when it's not the bride.

Our Potato Pam is always a loner and/or the outcast of the group. The childhood friend that doesn't know anyone else in the party outside of meeting them at the bachelorette weekend. One can only imagine what a blasty blast that must've been! Ha! Or she's someone the bride felt obligated to include.

Pam has zero input on anything and answers in a monotone "whatever you guys want" to any inquiry, from music preference to food choice. You'll spot her off to the side sighing occasionally and pouting like a naughty youngster with their nose in the corner. When others try to include her in the reindeer games she will undoubtedly recoil and sit out.

Funsies.

Our Potato isn't to be confused with **Rally Girl Rhonda**. Rhonda will start out the morning very quiet and segregate herself from the group, but it's not due to a lack of personality. Nope. She's trying to sober up from the night before! She was having so much fun after the rehearsal dinner that she forgot the main event wasn't happening until today. Whoops!

Pro Tip: Even if she is at the beginning of the lineup that the bride or wedding planner provided you, offer to push her back a bit. She needs to let the Tylenol and hair of the dog have time to kick in, and otherwise, you'll just end up having to fix the hair she laid on or the makeup she smeared.

Once Rhonda gets her hangover cure of choice and she is able to see straight again, she'll rally! It will be like a switch flipped and then she tends to mimic our Hype Girl Hailey more and more throughout the morning!

She's a good egg. She'll be ready for another round of debauchery just as soon as she gets the pain reliever of choice, carbs and coffee/water/bloody mary situation handled.

I'd like to end this chapter with a little story about another personality type that is near and dear to my heart. **The Biggest Fan,** otherwise known as the girl who thinks she's Lauren Conrad. I know that I said I'd start with the bad and wrap this chapter with the good but this particular character deserves to be the exclamation point at the end of the chapter. She's not necessarily 'bad' she's just a strong personality and eventually, every bridal beauty pro experiences a Lauren!

The Lauren Conrad the actress is a beautiful and talented individual. What this personality type doesn't understand is that there is only room for one actual Lauren Conrad on this earth and SHE isn't it.

This poor man's Lauren shows many, many photos of her favorite celebrity. Other BIggest Fan favorites include Carrie Underwood, Sophia Vergara, Hailey Bieber, Blake Lively, Kate Middleton and Meghan Markle. All stunning inspirations and amazing muses. It's when it becomes unrealistic or obsessive that it's a problem.

This particular Lauren shared more than a dozen photos of The Lauren Conrad. All in completely different looks. Hair up, hair down. Bold smokey eye, natural glam. Top knot, low pony to the side. Cat Eye liner and a red lip, understated eye and a sheer lipgloss. Casual, formal. Literally, all the things.

Clearly I could see from a mile away that I was being set up for failure. With each photo she shared, I'd ask "What do you like about this look?"

Her reply was always, "I dunno. She looks so pretty though!"

Help her out, Carleana! Help yourself!

"I really like these soft glam waves but I'm concerned that they won't stay all day because of the pending rain and humidity."

She responded with, "Oh, I would never wear glam waves! I like my hair in beachy waves if I wear it down."

Reroute.

I'm a quick study and was realizing I needed to ask specific questions about each feature of the hair or makeup. I then asked, "Oh. Well, what do you like about the makeup in this photo? I thought you wanted to stay pretty light and natural? This particular look is more heavy glam than what we've talked about so far."

"I hate the red lipstick in this picture but I dunno...I thought she looked pretty otherwise."

"Well, we can use this as an inspiration look. I can keep your skin fresh and dewy and skip the red lipstick. How do you feel about using the black, cat eye, liquid eyeliner in this picture? All the other looks you've shown me were softer and a bit more bridal."

"I hate black liner on my eye shape. It always looks terrible! I *only* wear brown liner and NEVER a liquid." So matter of fact and sure that she knows what she wants. So long as it's something she can say she duplicated from The Lauren Conrad's catalog of looks apparently?

She shuffled through all the pictures again and pulled a completely different inspo photo of The Lauren Conrad. This particular paparazzi picture was of her on the street in a casual sundress. Her makeup had a lot of soft pink shades and her hair was tousled, wavy and mostly down.

"Maybe I like this one better," she said, knowing she didn't believe herself any more than I did.

"Are you liking the blush tones?" I asked.

"Eeww! You mean like pink? No! I don't *do* pink! Why do you think she's wearing pink makeup in this?" She questioned while scowling and looking me up and down.

I returned with, "Because she is." It was all I had left to give.

And that, my friends, is pretty much how the entire conversation went.

In the end, I gave her some soft beach waves and used two bobby pins - because that's specifically what The Lauren Conrad said she did in an article/blog. And naturally, that's the *only* way that we could possibly pin *this* Lauren's thick, long, heavy locks back out of her face! She actually unpinned her hair at one point because she was sure I had snuck an extra pin in there to secure it, and then she repinned it herself (which looked amateur hour as all hell), showing both of *her* pins in full view. I saw Lauren's poorly pinned hair and I looked away.

Sometimes we have to pick our battles and this was not the hill I was going to die on that day.

This concludes our list of Bride Tribe Personality Types.

Now, you may be thinking, 'What the sh!t?! Why is Carleana telling us these crazy stories? Is she trying to add to our wedding morning stylist anxieties??!'

The answer is, of course, no.

Most of your wedding parties won't be cringy or potato-y; what I am trying to do is prepare you for the worst case scenarios. These are just some of the types I have encountered in my 20 plus years of doing this. No matter what, if you find yourself in a less than ideal situation, you can navigate it and take comfort in the fact that it will be short-lived.

As you move forward in your career with your marketing funnel, pricing, and social media presence on point, you'll be able to be more selective with who you take on as a client.

Cheers to less problematic bridal parties and more Haileys, Lanas, Mommas and Rhondas in your chair!

Things to ponder:

- What is your best case scenario for a bridal party vibe?

- What is your worst case scenario for a bridal party vibe?

- What can you do to attract more of your dream bridal parties?

- Have you ever dealt with the Biggest Fan/Lauren Conrad syndrome in a bridal party?

- How would you explain that an inspiration photo had pink in it if they didn't recognize it?

- How do you stay up to date with trends so that you're 'in the know' for a Beauty Guru Becky?

LEGALLY-SCHMEGALLY TYPE STUFF:

The Things You Need to Know

"Being good in business is the most
fascinating kind of art."
-Andy Warhol

Let's get nerdy.

Traditionally, we have all been told that creative thinkers use the right side of their brain and critical thinkers use the left. Well, we as entrepreneurs need to be able to hone in on both.

According to webmd.com ...

Left-brained strengths include language, math, and analytical thinking.

Right-brained strengths include expression, emotional intelligence, and imagination.

According to the Left Brain vs. Right Brain Dominance Theory, the right brained thinkers are intuitive and creative. No surprise here, most hair stylists live in the right brained hemisphere. We use our hands and create new things. We use color theory and personal connections, not arithmetic or trigonometry in our day to day grind.

According to the same theory, people that are left brained are strong critical thinkers and use logic and numbers to make most decisions. Most left-brained thinkers would be horrified to peek into the organized chaos we, hair stylists, call a filing system. Or is that just me?

Like many things in psychology, this over-generalized concept has been written off as more of a myth than a theory by modern medicine. The Left Brain Right Brain Dominance Theory doesn't take into consideration that humans use both sides of their brain for different daily functions.

As inaccurate as this outdated theory may be, it doesn't mean that having a better understanding of our strengths and weaknesses isn't beneficial.

Although as a demographic hairstylists and makeup artists lean toward the right-brained ideology, we need to tap into the left side occasionally. Important things like running our business and filing taxes certainly lean more left brained. We need to use both sides of our brain in order to run a successful bridal beauty business... or any business for that matter. Being creative often gives us a huge disadvantage, but we creatives need to take the reins and change that narrative for our own good!

Obviously, I would love to live in the fantasy world where I get to do all the fun artsy things 24/7 and never deal with the mundane numbers, emails, and math yuckiness. But here we all find ourselves at the intersection of art and commerce. Here in the real world we have to embrace the other side of things and put our left brained skills to work.

Don't worry, I'm not about to suggest I know diddly about all of the legalities of filing your taxes correctly or all the business operation procedures where you live. I hire the professional accountants, bankers, and lawyers to do all the heavy lifting and numbers for me. However, I do want to give you a jumping off point to help you get started.

Get ready for some very vague, generalized, legally-schmegally type stuff...

Please note: This chapter is meant to point you in the right direction NOT to be used as a substitute for actual professional legal/banking/tax advice!!

In the great state of Michigan, I possess a cosmetology license which certifies me to legally perform hair, skin, and nail services on the general public. I have a bi-yearly licensing application and fee renewal that I must submit to LARA (Licensing and Regulatory Affairs) in order to stay current. Different states = different requirements. Some are annual and some require continued education hours. Be sure to check what qualifications are needed for your business location. I rent a salon suite and have it registered with LARA as well.

In addition to my cosmetology and rental licenses, I also have an LLC (Limited Liability Company) and my own DBA (Doing Business As). An LLC is a hybrid legal entity, having characteristics of both a corporation and a partnership or sole proprietorship. Most companies' DBA is different from their LLC.

Redken is a DBA. They likely do not file their taxes as 'Redken' because they're owned by L'Oréal Group, and that, my friends, is all entirely more complex than my sweet lil operation!

Banking can also be overwhelming. Opening a business account is important because banks and credit unions provide advantages that they may not offer personal accounts. Business banking also bleeds into filing your business taxes. I funnel my business account into my personal account by my accountant that renders a W-2 at the end of the year, so that I am paying into Social Security, income taxes, and everything else throughout the calendar year. I know many salon friends who pay it all in one lump sum at tax season. I also have salon friends that file their taxes quarterly. Some file a 10-99, and others have partnerships and file a K-1 or 10-65.

Bottom line is that in the world of banking and taxes you need to speak to a pro. I'm not that pro. There are hundreds of ways to structure your finances correctly. You need to assess what's best for you and your entrepreneurial business after speaking with someone in the financial industry that can help you to understand the pros and cons of each option.

Lastly, in order to protect my beauty business, I also have business insurance. This insurance is different from health insurance. This protects my *business* specifically. If someone got hurt or wanted to sue me for a refund after services rendered, my insurance company would back me and my business. I'm protected in the event of the unthinkable to make sure my family's livelihood isn't compromised and my sweet lil' business can survive. Ask your insurance agency for details on protecting you and your business where you live and work.

Puh-leese flex that left brain muscle and check with the proper licensing department in your country/state/county/province/township/etc. Make sure that you're meeting all legal requirements for your business location. Do the research and figure out what's best for you and your business.

I know all of this seems daunting but I promise once you are set up you barely have to think about any of it ever again. Most of this, if not all of it, can be taken care of online. It can be overwhelming, but it's necessary. Just do the thing.

Piano, Piano.

Okay, enough of the Ted Talk!

To-do list:

- Research what type of licensing is required for you to run your Bridal Beauty Business where you live and work. File the paperwork needed.

- Find out what type of insurance you need to have to protect you and your new business. Get it.

- Do you identify as more right or left brained, and how do you plan to make up for the skills that you're not naturally inclined to?

*PS: I AM A HAIRSTYLIST AND BUSINESS OWNER NOT A LAWYER OR TAX PROFESSIONAL. ALL OF THE THINGS IN THIS CHAPTER ARE A GENERALIZATION AND ARE MEANT TO HELP GUIDE YOU TOWARD FINDING THE ANSWERS FOR YOURSELF. THIS CHAPTER IS IN NO WAY A REPLACEMENT FOR LEGAL OR TAX ADVICE. DO THE RESEARCH NECESSARY TO PROTECT YOU AND YOUR BUDDING BUSINESS. IF YOU COULD PLEASE NOT SUE ME IT WOULD BE GREATLY APPRECIATED.

THANK YOU.

WHAT COMES AROUND
GOES AROUND:

#Trending

As I'm sitting here eyeballs deep in this year's bridal season, I keep catching myself reflecting on the trends of the past. I'm fascinated with everything that surrounds the beauty industry being so cyclical. Everything comes and goes and comes back again.

The good, the bad, and all the things we once thought were ugly, will be re-worked, re-imagined, and brought back as 'new'. Hello, high-rise mom jeans! I'm talkin' to you!

Case in point; Eyebrows! We have gone from pencil thin in the 1920's to Brooke Shields in the 1980's and back and forth a dozen times, to bring us to our current brow climate.

Back in the first few years of working with brides, if I came anywhere near their brows with a pencil or filler they recoiled and gasped, "What are you doing?!" with wild eyes and distrust. It was almost as though I was going to use a black Sharpie on their face. I would then have to calmly explain that it's a light blonde, matte shadow that just fills the natural brow in slightly. Everyone photographs better with a little brow saturation and definition, I promise.

This is a stark contrast to the current full, thick brow fashion trend where brides sit in my chair for makeup and say 'I like a dark, defined brow' before we even get started. By the way, I think some of my current brides would be just fine with the

Sharpie idea! We're also starting to see the 'fluffy' brow trend. This is a lot less dark and severe than a few years ago but instead focuses on brushing the brow hair upward to show off their length.

Gowns are not exempt from the fashion shifts from one era to the next. Not all that long ago it seemed every bride wore a mermaid cut. Before that a full ball gown. Now we're seeing sleeve options with every gown no matter what the cut. Many brides opt to change dresses between the ceremony and reception, or at a minimum, bustle their train and ditch the veil. Others add or subtract a cape, gloves, sleeves, skirt, etc, before their reception entrance.

"Fashions fade, style is eternal."

-Yves Saint Laurent

Another shift in bridal trends is the popular season to say 'I do'. I believe there is a strong connection to the color pallets people want to use and the season they choose to wed.

I know that the market and popular seasons are going to differ from one region or country to another. Much of this depends on more than just color palette and popularity. These are just the norms that I have noticed first hand in the midwest, and Michigan specifically.

If a couple gets married in the fall, there is a solid possibility that they are drawn to warm earthy tones or deep plums or reds. Lots of burnt orange and chocolate browns tend to be used in autumn as well.

When I was new to the bridal business, I booked mostly spring and early summer weddings. About ten years ago, I saw a huge swing toward late summer and fall weddings. My weekends were packed from late August through November with bridal parties. At this same time, I had very few spring and early summer weddings. Pastels were not the 'in' color when I had a lack of spring bookings.

I've watched the 'hair mass' migrate from the high crown of the head, down to the nape, over to the side for an asymmetrical look, and back again. When I use the term 'bulk of hair' or 'hair mass' I'm referring to the place in the upstyle that has the most hair, AKA the bun or chignon.

We've incorporated braids in recent years, when in past years they were considered juvenile. Every fad or vogue trend will come into the spotlight for a time, fade into the background, and then reappear years later.

When planning their wedding, I think every bride, at some point thinks, "Is this *too* trendy? Am I going to look back in twenty years and wonder why I chose such a hideous *blankity-blank*?"

The answer is almost certainly, yes! But that's okay!! Everyone made fun of 'sea foam green' and 'peach' for years. Now the designers have renamed them and we call those colors 'blush' or 'dusty rose' and 'sage' or 'mint'! What was once 'country blue' is now 'desert blue'. Most of us embrace it and consider it new and fresh! Every bride should do what makes them feel gorgeous, trends be damned!!

Veils? I've noticed a huge shift in how brides have approached their veil choice and placement. For a long time my bride's hair was piled high and structured up top. Almost out of necessity, the veil was spilling out from beneath the bulk of hair. The veils were made of tulle exclusively and reached to approximately elbow or fingertip length.

About twelve years ago a lot of brides went without a veil altogether. We also went through a short retro, bird cage veil era about ten years ago. I still love that look by the way!

Currently, brides are opting for more fullness and length when it comes to their veils and wearing them above the hair mass, rather than below. Many modern brides are wearing veils for the ceremony and removing them for the reception. Thanks to the recent royal weddings, no doubt, we've seen a lot of cathedral length veils cascading down to the floor, and then many additional yards behind the bride.

Tiaras? You were probably an early to mid 2000's bride! It seemed that every bride wanted a very clean, polished pile of barrel curls at the crown of her head with a tiara perched just in front. Remember my unique bride that chose to adorn her hair with grandma's favorite brooch? Being a sentimental fool myself, I love this idea!

Baby's Breath in your hair? Many people associate the delicate, little white puffs as an out of date late 1980's to early 1990's fad. If you got hitched between 2015 and 2017 you were likely a part of the mason jar and baby's breath era. It was so simple and sweet, and went well with the beginning of the fashionable barn wedding phase. Succulents were an even more recent trend and I've seen them everywhere from centerpieces, wedding cakes, boutonnieres and bouquets, to adorning the bride's hair.

Over the last few years, things are softer, a little more undone, and low at the nape. Many brides love the romantic tendrils that seem to fall effortlessly. They like the whimsy that surrounds that entire look. One bride described her perfect wedding hair as being "classically-boho", which I think fits many bridal vibes right now!

Currently, in the 2023/2024 wedding season, we are seeing the french-twist and midi-bun have their moment again. It's a not too high, not too low option. The bulk of hair is mid-head and is resting just at the occipital bone in the center back.

Another return from the past is the hair bow, or actually *all* bows! I've seen bows adorning hair, as well as bridal gowns, and even wedding cakes! Like I mentioned earlier, everything that comes around, goes around; we're also seeing a lot of bridal gowns with sleeves. Not dainty little cap sleeves like in the not so distant past. I'm referring to the full 1980's, Princess Diana, poofy sleeves. Go big or go home!! I could try matching the size of the sleeve to the hair-bulk in the future - thoughts? And prayers?

"I look like a snow beast!"

-Toula, My Big Fat Greek Wedding

On the other end of the spectrum, we're also seeing a lot of ultra chic, runway-inspired, sleek, low knots. Classic, polished, and pretty. An understated bridal look that, as with all things, will soon be dated and replaced with another fashion trend.

I've been asked many times what my favorite updo is. I think if I *had* to answer it would be, "whatever's next." Due to the ever shifting beauty and fashion industries, we are all victim to 'what's next'.

It's exciting to play around and see what new and innovative techniques you can cultivate. After doing my tenth low knot of the wedding season in a row, it starts to feel a bit stale. It's fun to have a bride show an inspo pic of something I've never done before or haven't done in eons! It's what keeps me creative and helps me stay fresh! I embrace trends and the brides that bring me new ideas. I have to tackle them one at a time and from the inside out. Sometimes I have to play around a bit to achieve the desired finished look. It's fun to conquer a new style or reclaim an old style!

In the end, as professional hair stylists and beauty professionals, our job is to help the bride feel like the most gorgeous version of herself on her wedding day. We need to help her find the perfect hairstyle to compliment her overall bridal look, including but not limited to, her dress, jewelry, face shape, and hair texture. When the bride gets to see her overall vision of herself come together on her wedding day, it's pure joy!

In 2005, we got married out on my family's property and I really wanted the reception in the old 1850's hay barn. My parents thought I was nuts. It wasn't a thing yet. Nowadays, couples pay top dollar to rent large, bougie barns to say their nuptials.

What can I say? I was ahead of my time.

My color palette was black and white. I got asked over and over "Won't that look like a funeral?" with a hint of disgust lingering on their lips.

"What's your accent color, though?" asks a confused family member.

"Black." I'd reply.

"But what *other* color are you using?"

"White." I'd reply.

They'd squint their eyes and cock their heads to the side in bewilderment. Often looking up and to the left trying to picture this gothic idea of a black wedding in their mind's eye.

If you know me at all, you know it's not a stretch to assume that I would choose a colorless wedding motif. It's in my character. I loved it and don't regret it, and damn it, I was the bride and did my thang.

I encourage every bride to embrace what they want and be happy with the choices that they make.

We want every bride to LOVE her own reflection!

Contemplation Points:

- What are some of your favorite current trends?

- What is one wedding trend you don't miss?

- What's a bridal trend you'd love to see return?

- Have you regretted some of the fashion choices you've made over the years?

- Has there ever been a trend you just couldn't stand when it was all the rage? What was it?

WHAT'S NEXT?

Thinking Ahead...

By now I'm sure you've come to terms with the fact that I'm not big on excuses. You'll find that this chapter is no different. I'm a 'take the bull by the horns' and make it happen kinda gal. You're in charge of your own destiny. Waiting for others to make things happen for your career is as crazy as sitting at a stop sign and waiting for traffic. Take this as your sign, glaringly obvious as it may have been throughout this entire book, to go out and make your own luck. Build the relationships, post the pics, walk the walk, and do the things.

A year from now I want you to sit down and look back over all the questions that you've answered within the pages of this book. Much like a time capsule, you'll be amazed at the progress you've made in such a short period of time!

Now that you have your bridal beauty business up and functioning, what's next?

Maybe you've been offered a spot on a beauty team or have been recruited by an HMUA agency. Those can both be amazing opportunities!

Make sure to read the contracts thoroughly and confirm that they'll be a good fit for your lifestyle and your business. Make sure that their company's vision aligns with yours and that their price points are comparable too.

Have you thought about stepping back and working weekends

exclusively in order to have more family time?

Have you contemplated helping to teach your skills to other hair stylists? There are amazing opportunities to guest teach at shows and cosmetology schools all the time, you just have to look for them.

Maybe your next step is diving into solely providing bridal beauty services and stepping away from your full time gig as a hair stylist providing cuts, color and so on during the week? Or are you ready to take your career in a different direction altogether and open your very own salon or start your own beauty team?

> "Self confidence is a super power.
> Once you start to believe in yourself,
> magic starts happening"
> -Unknown

Whatever your next step is I hope that you can tackle it with the confidence you've gained within the pages of this book.

If you've read this book cover to cover and executed everything I've shared with you; you're set up with a fully functioning marketing funnel, you have your contracts and branding in place and you know you have the skill set to charm the pants off of any wedding vendor or bride that comes your way! I wish nothing but the best for you and your business! The sky's the limit!!

Happy Pinning!!

XO
Carleana

Questions to end with:

- Once you're successful, I mean truly successful, what comes next?

- What does your success look like to you?

- Does success mean having hundreds of bookings annually?

- Does it mean owning a salon or a bridal business with a team of stylists beneath you?

- Does it mean you have multiple vacations a year?

- More time off with family and friends?

- Define, in your own terms, what success means for you and your business.

CONCLUSION:

Final Thoughts

The perfect time doesn't exist, so let's aim for the best time instead.

Today is the absolute best time to get started on your bridal beauty business! Why, do you ask? Because you know more today than you did yesterday, and after completing this book and filling out the questions at the end of each chapter, you now possess the outline to make your dreams a reality.

Only your own fears and self doubt can hold you back at this point.

Inexperience is an excuse. All the What-If-Monsters are also excuses. We can be crippled by fears and self doubt. We have to work through the negative what-ifs and replace them with positive ones.

Instead of "What if it doesn't work out?" or "What if I fail?" Let's start asking ourselves "What if it *does* work?" and "What if I *do* succeed?"

The world of freelance entrepreneurship can be overwhelming and leave you feeling vulnerable. Nothing great or worth doing has ever started in someone's comfort zone. If things like owning your own business were easy, everyone would do it. There wouldn't be any huge fortune 500 companies because everyone would be working for themselves, right? FYI: even those giant retailers had to start somewhere. They didn't just open their doors and have 1000's of locations overnight. They started small and step by step grew into the mega stores we now know today.

"...no such thing as perfect..."
-Brené Brown, The Gifts of Imperfection

At the time of publishing, I had been working on my book for well over a decade and a half. For one reason or another - see 'excuses' in the lingo glossary - I never seemed to get very far.

It started as a 'tell all' of sorts. The silly and sometimes risky stories that every hairstylist is privy to throughout their career. The "who said whats" of the bustling metropolis East Lansing. My working title was 'Stories from Behind My Chair.' If only I had less excuses for myself sooner I could've had that title for myself. C'est la vie.

I ended up pivoting my thought process by the time I had written and rewritten chapter 227 ... Partially due to the fact that it was morphing into a gossip rag and the only 'who's who' involved were a few local tv personalities, local business owners, and a handful of Michigan State University athletes, coaches, and alumni. Interesting to Mid-Michigan residents, sure, but the book had zero purpose beyond that.

My book wasn't sharing knowledge or wisdom. I wasn't helping in any way. I was having to disguise names for anonymity. (I still had to do that in this book!) Even if you were invested in my titillating collection of short stories, I wasn't feeling fulfilled. It left me asking myself, 'What's the point'? and 'Who the hell is going to read this?'

To what benefit would my book be to the reader?

Pivot.

Salon tips and tricks?

Pivot.

How to build a beauty business...

Better.

Let's get more specific, Carleana. How I built a successful bridal beauty business...

Found it!

Now that we're closing in on the end of my book, the way I see it, you have two choices.

One: Continue with trials and errors

or

Two: Get results.

It's okay to have questions or doubts, just don't let them cripple you. If you're waiting for permission to start your own freelance beauty business, here you go! Permission granted! You just rubbed the magic lamp three times and out popped your genie! And no, that's not a euphemism. You can now pursue your dreams!!

"I'm the same as you, just a few steps ahead."
-Matt Rudnitsky

Remember I was once where you are currently, at one point or another. I was the cosmetology graduate fresh in the beauty world with no specific direction. I was the stylist with 5 years of experience and fumbling to build my referral base. I was the salon updo queen that sat and waited for the busy bus to drop off more bridal clients. I was the social media stylist throwing hashtags in the dark hoping something would stick.

But... This isn't about me and my business. This is about you and yours.

> "The future belongs to those who believe
> in the beauty of their dreams."
> -Eleanor Roosevelt

Don't trivialize your accomplishments no matter how big or small. One day you'll look back on where you are now. You'll recognize the many milestones you've met over your career, and you will smile knowing you've accomplished things that you once only dreamt of.

I hope that you take this information and run with it. I hope that you surpass what I've done in my career! I hope to sit down with you one day, have a cup of coffee (or wine) and have you 'wow' me by teaching me a few things about this amazing industry.

Follow the steps. Do the work. Accomplish the things, meet the goals and live the dream!

ACKNOWLEDGMENTS:

My people-

You know who you are and you know that I love you!! I couldn't do this life without every single one of you!

Family- husband, kids, parents...

The biggest most heartfelt thank you to my family.
My Mom and Dad have always taught me the importance of hard work. I learned from your example that dedication to any task always pays off in the end.
My husband and girls continue to be a wealth of love and support throughout my career and especially while I ignored them for hours on end while writing and editing this book! I often found myself hiding in quiet corners of the house to get just a little more work done. "Leave mom alone for a little bit, she's working on her book" was an all too common phrase. Please know that it was appreciated and didn't go unnoticed! Now that it's finished and published we all deserve to celebrate! Wudge you the most! XO

Brides- Past, current and future ....

Without the hundreds of brides entrusting me with their hair and makeup over the years, these pages would be blank. You have all given me many experiences to now share with the beauty industry. I can never repay you enough for that! Thank you and may you always feel as gorgeous as you did on your wedding day!!

Clients- Past, current, future...

To my salon clients that have continuously supported me throughout my career, I thank you! Thank you for laughing and celebrating life's big and little moments with me. Thank you for feeling comfortable enough to share your ups and downs. Thank you for letting me be a part of your lives as well as remaining a huge part of mine.

Jackee-

You are one of my most vibrant cheerleaders and the founder and sole member of my fan club! You were one of the first people to know about this lil project of mine and have always been a beacon of support. You are my chosen family and I love all our many traditions and memories made. Looking forward to more travel, laughs and milestones! More than all the fishies in the sea!

Salon Family- Past and Present...

I'm talking to all of you, owners, receptionists and stylists. I can't even begin to list everyone, but please know that you've all made an impact on me. We often seem to see each other more than our own families. You've all taught me so much over the years, I feel like I have the most random database of knowledge due to each of your unique perspectives and expertise! Thank you for your friendship and all the countless breakroom laughs!!

The Joni-

Thank you for being my work wife over the past two decades and always keeping me on my toes! Salon life wouldn't be the same without you in it.

Local Authors-

Both Cindy Kline and Lori Spielman are time salon clients that I have had the privilege of knowing long before they were successful, published authors! Although they both write in completely different genres from myself or one another, they are a continuous inspiration!

Thank you both for sharing your writing journeys with us at the salon!!

To support these amazing mid Michigan women, please visit

www.lorinelsonspielman.com

www.cindykline.com

Tech Support-

As I have mentioned previously, I am one of the least tech-savvy people I know. That being said, I owe my sanity to Pat Dally, Chris Beaudrie, Sarah Hendrickson and an honorable mention to my husband, Shaun! Thank you for helping me with glitches, cover art specifics and jpeg vs pdf oddities!

Sarah Hendrickson-

Last, but certainly not least, my humble editor extraordinaire! Somehow, you were able to keep this distracted squirrel on task. Not only did you take time away from your family to help me, but you also kept my writing P.C. and understood my voice and message. Knowing your brilliant acting and comedic background, I was always proud to get you to laugh while reading my rough drafts. I know you don't give those laughs up easily! There isn't much in this book that doesn't have your polish on it. From the bottom of my heart, thank you. You will forever be one of my all time favorite ninjas!!

LINGO:

a Glossary-

Below is a list of words, phrases and jargon that are used throughout this book that may or may not need further clarification. They are not listed alphabetically because it didn't seem to make sense, instead I have chosen to arrange the terms in a somewhat organized chaos. Some of the lingo used are industry standards and some are my own 'isms'... enjoy!

* * *

Beauty Business= Anything done within the scope of the beauty industry to thrive and make a living. Hair stylist, salon owner, social media influencers, makeup artists, beauty educators, and many more professions fall under this category.

Entrepreneur= A person who organizes and operates any enterprise, especially a business, usually with considerable initiative and risk. i.e. an employer, founder, administrator, critical thinker, promoter, executer, marketer, owner, pioneer and doer of all things necessary to build and retain a successful business.

Styled Shoot= A photoshoot that is set up to showcase the

talents of the crew. Everyone involved brings their creative best and collaborates to make a faux wedding day experience that can be captured by the photographer. Often used for publication and always used as social media and promotional materials. Mood boards are generally provided to provide context and the wedding professionals involved get to flex their creative muscles.
aka: stylized shoot

Mood Board - A visual representation or collage of images and text that help explain a mood or vibe of an upcoming project. Often the board includes sample dresses, color schemes, jewelry, buzz words and more for the vendors involved to prepare for the upcoming project.

Bridal Stylist= A hair stylist that specializes specifically in the art of beautifying brides on their wedding day.

MUA= acronym: MakeUp Artist

HMUA= acronym : Hair and MakeUP Artist

Call time= The expected time of arrival for all participants for an event. Ready to work and/or be worked on.
i.e. the performance starts at 12:00pm: crew call time is 9:00am and dancer's call time is 10:00am.

Booking=Referring to any arrangement made between two or more parties at a particular time in the future. Including but not limited to photoshoots, weddings, commercials, stage performances and runway shows. i.e. The bride signed the contract to secure her booking.

Ghosting= Often used in the dating world when one party stops responding to the other. Used in this industry/book when a potential client corresponds repeatedly, asks a ton of questions (often wasting your time) then stops responding completely which leaves you not knowing if they intend to book or not.

Evergreen Material= Content that stays fresh or 'green' for consumers despite it's publication date. Material that lasts over time and requires very little or no updating years down the road. i.e. A blogger posting about eyebrow trends in 2015 has some updating to do because the trend has since changed, it isn't evergreen.

Behind the Chair= Work that is specifically done on clients. Whether you're performing an upstyle or a color and cut, those are behind the chair services.

Commission Salon= As a stylist in a commission salon you work for the owner and receive a W2 at the end of the year to file your taxes. You have very few write-offs and work to build your clientele. In exchange for your percentage of each service rendered (sometimes 50/50 but varies on location) the owner takes care of all bills including water, electricity etc... and provides cleaning crew, a receptionist for bookings as well as all products and marketing materials like business cards.

Chair Rent Salon= Often the next step after working in a commission based salon. You rent your chair and provide your own products (this may vary depending on the salon's setup but often you purchase your own color, bowls, tint brushes, styling products and wet bar inventory) Still configured like a traditional salon, usually with a front desk and receptionist.

Salon Suite= A small studio space with a private entrance to render beauty services in a private, curated space all your own. Often the layout of a suite rental building is set up like an office building or co-op that has many different entrances to each suite via a main hallway. As a suite rental/small business owner you provide all marketing materials and take care of all booking responsibilities. Best suited for a seasoned stylist that no longer wants to be employed by a traditional commission or chair rental salon and wants full control over their branding and overall client experience. Often called 'studios' as well.

Salon Studio= See 'Salon Suite' above.

On Location= When the services rendered are done in a place other than a traditional salon setting often requiring travel. i.e. a wedding venue, hotel, church basement, grandma's kitchen, etc…

Updo= The American version of Up Styling. The catch all noun for any formal hair style that is pinned up or back including but not exclusive to buns, knots, braids, chignons, french twists, etc…

½ Up= A formal style only taking ½ of the hair (or less) up to be pinned or secured in place, leaving the rest down to show off the length of the hair. An alternative to leaving all the hair down in its entirety. Also appropriate when a client is more comfortable with her hair down but wants to look more formal and finished.

Bridal Preview= Formally known as the 'bridal trial' or 'practice updo'. An appointment set up weeks or months prior to the wedding date to practice the bridal hair and/or makeup look wanted by the bride. Useful tool to make sure both parties are on the same page for the wedding day look.

Bangs= The fringe or front pieces framing one's face. (American)

Fringe= The bangs or front pieces framing one's face. (Australian/UK) See what I did there?

Bridal Kit= Anything and everything you bring with you as a professional hair and/or makeup artist. All of your products and tools needed to provide services for a booking, photoshoot or wedding should fit within an easily carryable tote bag or vessel.

Hair Bling= Referring to anything that adorns a bridal look, other than a veil. Flowers, sparkly bits, tiaras, crowns, pins, etc… (I also use 'dazzly bits' to reference the same thing.)

Bobby Pin= double pronged hair pin made of wire approximately

1.5 inches in length, used to help secure a formal up style. Prongs <u>do</u> touch at the ends.

Hairpin= double pronged wire about 1.5 inches in length used for light detail work in formal hair styling, not suitable for tight or heavy pinning. Prongs <u>do not</u> touch at the ends.

Elastic= A small rubber band used to secure the hair in formal work. Typically found in clear, black or brown.

Hair Donut= A circular (hence the name) hair colored synthetic mesh used as padding to bulk up buns and other upstyles. Unseen beneath the hair. Commonly found in black, dark brown and blonde.

'Zilla= Pretty well explained in the 'Always a Bridesmaid' chapter but... a Zilla is anyone who sabotages the mojo of a wedding via obsessively self indulgent and negative behavior. (Also described as a nag, bucket dipper, drama queen or Karen.)

MOB= Mother Of the Bride

FOB= Father Of the Bride

Product Cocktailing= Any combination of hair products that a professional puts together like a prescription to achieve a specific bridal look for a specific client. Cocktailing can use two or more products, including but not exclusive to hairspray, mousse, gel, cream, wax, spray wax, dry shampoo, powder, pomade, lotions, potions, etc...

SuperMart= Not an actual physical place, it's my version of a big box store to cover all generic 'one stop shop' super stores instead of listing specific ones that are generally regional or country specific.

Caboodles= Popular late 80's /early 90's makeup case reminiscent of a tackle box. Used to organize anything from hair accessories, art supplies, makeup, and more. Available in many colorful options including rainbow hues, pastels, and sparkles.

Every youngster had a Caboodles case. Everyone.

MapQuest= A prehistoric version of GPS or GoogleMaps. It was actually quite revolutionary at the time. Before that we had literal state maps and atlases in our glove boxes. Ha! Imagine!! >Replaced the atlas and map options for road trips and car travel. Was launched in 1996 as the first commercial web mapping service. Revolutionary at the time. Eventually acquired by America Online in 2000. No longer a popular option much like TomTom and other devices have been replaced by apps like Google Maps amongst others coming to the market in more recent years.

Marketing Funnel= Your marketing funnel describes your customer's journey with you from beginning to end. From initially learning about you and your business all the way through purchasing your product or services.

Excuses= To remove the blame. i.e.: excuses are like asses, everybody has one. Don't excuse your life away.

What-if-monsters= All the little things in our heads (oftentimes completely fictitious) that get in the way of becoming successful. Also known as doubts and fears.

Naysayers= Negative Nancy types that hate to see other's successes. Will criticize any detail to remove positivity and reflect unneeded negativity. Also use: Cynic, killjoy, defeatist.

Hair-Mass= When I use the term 'bulk of hair' or 'hair mass' I'm referring to the bun or chignon. Where the majority of the hair is styled to sit on the head.

Tulle= A shear net like material made of soft silk, cotton or nylon. Often used in bridal gowns and veils.

Tiara= A half or partial crown traditionally worn high on the head. Often fixed with a comb.

Excuses= Everyone has one. "I'm too busy." / "I don't know

how." / "What if..." / "I'm not ready." ...all are unacceptable. The only person an excuse harms is yourself.
i.e. : An attempt to remove blame; a plea offered for a fault or for release from an obligation or promise.

Types of Veils:

Cathedral length= think royal weddings. Cathedral length veils are very long and spill onto the floor behind the bride for yards. Normally anywhere from 9 to 25 feet in length.

Birdcage= a short, structured veil that covers part of the face with a comb sitting on top of the head. Normally made of french netting or netted tulle; a wider weave much like fishnet stockings. A very retro 1940's look. (war time brides of this era had to use a minimalist approach due to the shortage of fabrics)

Elbow Length= As you may have guessed, this option hits at or near the bride's elbow. This is a great option for a traditional ball gown style dress because it stops at the waist line before the fullness of the skirt starts.

Fingertip= pretty self explanatory... a veil that drapes to roughly the length of your fingertips while standing with your arms falling down to either side.

Blusher=Traditional brides tend to love this bust grazing sheath of fine tulle that comes forward over the face as they walk down the aisle. Usually lifted by either the father of the bride or groom during the ceremony.

Mantilla= Also referred to as a 'spanish veil' ; sometimes another veil option made of a single layer of tulle and trimmed in lace. Worn draped over the head and framing the bride's face. Popular in Latin America and Spain and another nod to a vintage bridal vibe.

Ballerina= Another classic. Tulle that lands anywhere from knee to ankle and offers drama without the tripping hazard of a cathedral length veil.

Tiered Veil= This option is a layered look that is made up of two or more sheets of tulle at multiple lengths. Often one layer is pulled forward over the bride's face to act as a blusher for the ceremony.

Happiness= The quality or state of being happy. The attainment of what one considers good and cheerful. Also known as; good fortune; pleasure; contentment; joy; satisfaction; bliss.

REVIEWS:

"Carleana has been my go-to hair stylist for all things bridal! Her ability to create an artful and beautiful hair style, with seemingly no pause, is truly impressive. She is personable and warm, making each lady feel comfortable and at ease and is incredibly reliable. Carleana has continuously participated in creative bridal shoots, without hesitation, for the opportunity to do what she does best- create hair MAGIC! There's no doubt in my mind you will be utterly satisfied with Carleana's work!"

- Cayla Johnson, Becker's Bridal

"Carleana has worked with Pierre's for years, showcasing her phenomenal hair and makeup talents at every event and shoot. If you're looking for someone to book for your next gala or wedding, Carleana is your girl!"

Sarah, Pierre's Bridal

ABOUT THE AUTHOR

Carleana Delacruz

This is Carleana's first book. She has been a professional hairstylist for over two decades and continues to love her career! When she isn't behind the chair you'll find her spending time with her family and friends, traveling, cooking or enjoying a cup of coffee or a glass of wine. Carleana enjoys sharing her career experiences with other hairstylists. In Hairpins & Happiness: A Hairstylist's guide to Building a Successful Bridal Business she helps you outline all of the necessary steps to grow an entrepreneurial beauty business that you can be proud of!

To learn more about Hairpins & Happiness
and Carleana's work please visit

www.hairpinsandhappiness.com

and follow along @hairpinsandhappiness
#hairpinsandhappiness

NOTES:

space for notes, scribbles and to-do lists...

NOTES:

more space for doodles...

Made in the USA
Monee, IL
02 January 2024

50966813R00095